soR

oue

CHANGE

DEDICATION

To the memory of my mother, Fay Zoerner.

SORTING OUT CHANGE

GRANT BRECHT

PRENTICE HALL

Sydney   New York   Toronto   Mexico   New Delhi
London   Tokyo   Singapore   Rio de Janeiro

Aquisitions Editor: Kaylie Smith
Production Editor: Esperanza Egan
Copy Editor: Loretta Barnard
Cover design: Eilish Bouchier
Illustrations: David Egan

Typeset by Keyboard Wizards, Allambie Hts, NSW
Printed in Australia by Australian Print Group, Victoria

1 2 3 4 5 01 00 99 98 97

ISBN 0 7248 1119 2

National Library of Australia
Cataloguing-in-Publication Data

Brecht, Grant Phillip
  Sorting out change

  Includes index
  ISBN 0 7248 1119 2

  1. Change (Psychology). 1. Title.
  (Series : Sorting out life series).

158.1

Prentice Hall of Australia Pty Ltd, *Sydney*
Prentice Hall, Inc., *Englewood Cliffs, New Jersey*
Prentice Hall Canada, Inc., *Toronto*
Prentice Hall Hispanoamericana, SA, *Mexico*
Prentice Hall of India Private Ltd, *New Delhi*
Prentice Hall International, Inc., *London*
Prentice Hall of Japan, Inc., *Tokyo*
Simon & Schuster (Asia) Pte Ltd, *Singapore*
Editora Prentice Hall do Brasil Ltda, *Rio de Janeiro*

 PRENTICE HALL
A division of Simon & Schuster

CONTENTS

PREFACE

There is a very common saying these days that the only thing you can rely on to be constant is change! While I guess there is some truth in that, we need to be careful that we do not talk ourselves into a panic and begin to believe that change is a new phenomenon only experienced this decade.

There is no doubt at all that certain aspects of our lives and the things around us happen very quickly and at times are very difficult to keep up with. We need to be very aware of what these things are and how to buffer ourselves against them, otherwise our quality of life could be severely hampered. Yet, change has always been a part of life for all generations of human beings. Imagine the impact of the Industrial Revolution on the generations of that time. The early settlement of Australia by the British and other Europeans would have meant immense changes for both the settlers and the Aboriginal inhabitants for much of their life—in fact, I suppose some people would argue that those changes are still not complete!

Now of course, not all changes are happening out there in our environment—many actually happen within and to us. One that scares the hell out of many of us is the ageing process! The amount of change we go through in our lives due to this one phenomenon is quite staggering. We go from being dependent on others to being dependent on ourselves and then having others depend on us. We go through many physical changes as we go through life, and learning to accept them and deal with them effectively is critical.

We play many different roles in life, from being a child at school, to a young adult in the workforce, a lover, a parent, a sportsperson, a responsible citizen, a grandparent or a retiree. Moving between the various roles involves changes, some small and non-threatening; others require a larger leap and may appear more threatening and anxiety-producing.

While some changes we face are controllable, others are not. Some changes are impossible to predict or control. Does this mean we cannot cope as well with them, or that they will necessarily be more catastrophic in their consequences? No, of course not—if you have developed effective coping habits.

Not being able to adapt quickly and effectively to changes in our life circumstances can impact very negatively on our quality of life. We may remain trapped in the 'wasn't it great when' syndrome with all sorts of emotional consequences, or we may sabotage the changes or just feel worn out and give up.

Change, like any other challenge in life needs to be met head on, with proper preparation and planning, and with positive and solution-oriented attitudes and actions. This book will show you how to:

◆ develop an attraction to change where possible, rather than a resistance to it;

◆ understand why we allow change to bother us;

◆ be aware of the barriers to effective coping as we pass through the stages of dealing with change;

◆ develop effective coping strategies to deal with any form of change;

◆ handle someone who has difficulty dealing adaptively with change;

◆ know when you are a great manager of changes in your life.

Enjoy your reading, and enjoy the challenges of the many changes life will afford you.

Grant P Brecht

ACKNOWLEDGMENTS

Thanks to Kaylie Smith, Liz Thomas, Loretta Barnard and all the team at Prentice Hall Australia for showing their support for the *Sorting Out* series by working so industriously to produce these wonderful books.

To David Egan for his creative illustrations which have added so much to the presentation of the series.

Once again to my family for their support and encouragement throughout.

To the many friends and work colleagues who have been enthusiastic and interested in my desire to create this series of self-help books.

And finally my respect and best wishes to all of you who are shrugging off the victim role in life and taking the ownership for *Sorting Out* your life.

ABOUT THE AUTHOR

Grant is a Clinical Psychologist who lives and works in Sydney Australia. The first release of four books from the *Sorting Out* series were all written by Grant as are the books in this release, *Sorting out Change* and *Sorting out Relationships*. He is a sought-after presenter and speaker who is passionate about the topics he writes about. Grant is well known for his radio and television appearances assisting people in sorting out their lives. He is a Director of CORPsych—a clinical and organisational psychological consultancy providing employee assistance programs, counselling and training services to companies and individuals across Australia and the Asia Pacific region. Grant has a unique ability to impart information aimed at assisting people to learn psychological self-help techniques in a very practical and enjoyable manner, as those of you who have read his other books will know.

Look for other books by this very popular author of the *Sorting Out* series. They are available in all good book shops.

ABOUT THE SERIES

This is the second release of books in the *Sorting Out* series. The first four are still very popular and there are now two more to add to your collection.

A wise person once remarked that 'Life is not about having no problems, but rather about being able to resolve them when they occur'.

The *Sorting Out* series has been written to assist each of us to do just that—to sort out those everyday life challenges that confront every one of us. Whether it be ongoing and unnecessary worry and anxiety, an inability to plan and set goals in life, low self-esteem and a poor self image, too many perceived demands with too few coping strategies, too much change and uncertainty, or an inability to communicate well with others and hence poor relationships, the books in this series will be of immense practical value and benefit.

Our modern lifestyles are demanding and the rapid rate of social and technological change is placing enormous pressures on most of us. Quality of life is determined by how well we predict and rise to the challenges which are placed before us on our journey through life, and by our ability to communicate effectively. Effective communication is about remaining flexible, adaptable, rational, positive and solution-orientated no matter what is happening in our lives.

This very practical and relevant series will assist everyone in developing awareness of the issues and topics covered: how we know if change is a problem for us, including the signs and symptoms, and what we can do about it; how we know when we are successful and where to seek further assistance if we need to; how to live with someone with that particular concern or problem.

The techniques and self-help procedures outlined by the author in the series are drawn from the latest research into the most effective approaches for dealing with the problems and hassles of every-day living.

The books in the *Sorting Out* series make a wonderful library of the most practical life skills which can be applied to many of life's challenges. There will be more to follow.

CHAPTER 1

Change, change and more change

I see not what is and ask why
I see what is not, and ask why not.

John F. Kennedy

That rather small and notable quote by the former President of the United States of America really does sum up our 'modern' thinking about change and the need for change. We tend to use the concept of change to indicate our need to be progressive and forward thinking. Change is progress, change is creative, change leads to a better way, change means a better standard of living for all, and so change is necessary and it comes with a sense of urgency. We need to do it, and we need to do it now.

This is the way many people view change in their external circumstances, such as the work environment, technology, medical research and so on. However, change in a personal sense can often be seen as very undesirable. The ageing process, divorce or separation, a diagnosis of a nasty illness—these types of changes are all unwelcome and can be quite devastating to the individual involved. Of course the events in life just mentioned will bring a whole range of reactions from a whole range of different people. Some will feel challenged and stimulated, others will feel overwhelmed and frightened.

Why the different reactions to the same event or series of events? It is obviously to do with the psychological make-up of particular people. Distinctively, the beliefs they hold about the way the world *should* or *must* be, the amount of *control* they believe they have over events in their lives, past, present and future, the *relevant experiences* they have had in the past, and how these worked out, okay or not so okay.

The outcome of the experiences people have had dealing with previous changes in their lives is a crucial element because this then leads to people developing a *belief system* in their memory banks. The *belief system* is made up of our thoughts and perceptions about all previous life experiences and we then use this knowledge to weigh up the present events and situations we find ourselves in. Positive experiences usually lead to positive perceptions, while negative experiences will normally lead to negative perceptions and reactions from the person. So, what is stored in the person's *belief system* is very important in terms of their reactions to any changes happening in their lives, big or small.

We will deal a lot more with our *belief systems* throughout the book; however right now, I feel it would be very interesting to have a look at another period of history and see what changes were happening at that time. We know, of course, that people have always had to face and deal with personal changes such as ageing, death of loved ones, different roles in life, sickness, promotions at work and so on, but we are now hearing things like 'change has never been this pace', 'there has never been this degree of change before'. People who make these comments are, of course, referring to those larger systems of things in their environment such as technology, social norms, work practices, economic conditions and so on. Is this fact or fiction? It is fiction I'm afraid, which means we can't really get into a 'poor me' trip to try and cope due to the fact that life is so terrible now because of all these nasty changes that are going on. To illustrate why this is fiction and a myth, let's take a brief look at history around the time that famous soft drink, Coca-Cola was being born.

In 1881, George Beard wrote a book called *American Nervousness, Its Causes and Consequences*. In it, he talks about the general concern about a new disease characterised by neurotic, psychosomatic symptoms. He attributes this 'new disease', which he labelled 'neurasthenia', to the overwhelming pace of change that was sweeping America at that time. The rate of change was blamed on 'modern civilisation', especially industrialism and a revolution in transportation methods which brought major social and economical upheaval. He particularly talks about the steam engine which he states was designed to make work easier, but which had in fact resulted in more 'frantic lifestyles and in overspecialisation'. The answer to coping with the tremendous change and this new disease—why, Coca-Cola of course! In his unauthorised history of the great American soft drink, *For God, Country and Coca-Cola*, Mark Pendergrast notes that:

Coca-Cola emerged from this turbulent, inventive, noisy, neurotic new America. It began as a 'nerve tonic' like many others marketed to capitalise on the dislocations and worries of the day.

It is reported that in those early days there was enough cocaine in the soft drink so that the recommended one glass with each meal would keep your 'worries' away for the complete day.

These days of course, it would be considered a very maladaptive way of coping with the stresses and the uncertainties of change. However, it does testify to the fact that large numbers of people in the late nineteenth century were finding the changes in their environment difficult to cope with and were seeking methods to reduce the concerns and symptoms they were suffering.

So we can conclude from a quick glance at days gone by that change on the scale that we are experiencing in the 1990s is not a novel experience for human beings. But because we were not around in the 1880s, this type of comparison is not all that meaningful or helpful to our generations in terms of what we may have learnt from 'being there before'.

Even if we don't consider those major systems changes in our environments, but focus on the more personal changes such as ageing, death of a loved one or retrenchment from a job, it may be that this is the first time we have experienced such an event or perhaps we coped poorly the other times we experienced such things.

Will undesirable or unexpected changes suddenly disappear? I doubt it. Change is an unavoidable part of life. Whether within us or out there in our environment, change will be there. It will

4

haunt us and fill us with fear and trepidation, or it will invigorate and motivate us. At the end of the day it really depends on us. What do you want? Do you wish to be overcome with feelings of 'I can't cope, why is this happening to me, this is terrible'? Or do you want to accept the challenges head on, 'what's the best thing for me to do given this is happening, what choices do I have, how can I make the most out of this'? It is really going to be up to each and every one of us to decide which route we will take. Which route will you take? It's your decision, and your decision alone. Exciting isn't it? You have a choice. You can be the master or mistress of your own destiny.

Don't panic or despair, as this book is about assisting you in coping and sorting out this continuing saga. The following chapters will help you to come to grips with the nebulous yet sometimes very real and threatening aspects of the changes impacting on you and those around you.

SUMMARY

◆ Some changes are unwelcome.

◆ Our psychological make-up affects the way we react to change.

◆ Our *belief system* also determines our reactions to change.

◆ Human beings have always been confronted by change.

◆ How we cope with change is up to us! We have a choice.

CHAPTER 2

Why the need for change?

An interesting question! Why the need for change? I guess at times we have all felt that certain changes forced on us in the work environment were really just change for the sake of change. Things seemed to be working fairly well the way they were going, so why do things differently? The answer we generally get back of course, is that other competitors are doing things differently and if we don't keep up with the latest ways, we will then not be competitive. Yet, we may feel that the change is more to do with a new manager wanting to make his or her mark, 'jobs for the boys' or some other reason which is more orientated towards self-interest rather than what is best for the company. A rather common attitude expressed during periods of work change is 'we have done it all before and it didn't work then, so why will it work now?'.

So many of us will hold a rather negative and cynical attitude to change, perhaps in many of the areas that change can affect us. We may view the prospect of growing older as frightening and terrible with a real dread of not being as useful, youthful or as on the ball as we once were. Now we have a dilemma! You could argue that changes in the workplace may not have been necessary, and that the same changes were not happening to everyone. But what about ageing? It's happening to everyone. It can certainly be argued that it is unavoidable and natural, even though many of us may not like it.

There are indeed many dimensions to the phenomenon of change. It may be:

- desired or undesired;
- controllable or uncontrollable;
- gradual or immediate;
- useful or not useful;
- large or small;
- forced or voluntary.

How we react depends on the mixture of the above scenarios. If we desire the change, feel that it is controllable, that it can be implemented in a gradual manner and it is useful, we are likely to welcome and embrace the new direction or pursuit in our life. If, however, the change is forced, large, uncontrollable and seen to be not useful we will *resist* whatever is being implemented or suggested.

The amount of *resistance* we mount against the change or changes will have a lot to do with the amount of *importance* we place on the particular event or happening in our life.

Any event in life will fall into one of four categories. It will either be:

- important and controllable;
- important and uncontrollable;
- unimportant and controllable; or
- unimportant and uncontrollable.

The controllability of the change affects our emotional reaction to the event and how long that reaction lasts. The more uncontrollable the event is seen to be will have an increasing effect on our levels of anxiety, apprehension and fear. However, the perceived importance of the event will have a direct effect on our level of resistance to the change. The more important the event, the more resistance there will be, if the change is not seen as desirable.

Let's now consider those common changes we are faced with throughout our life.

THE AGEING PROCESS

Fairly hard to escape this one, no matter how much we may like to! Of course there are a multitude of changes that we need to face as we age, including:

- *Different roles and expectations*—for different age groups, such as being a child, a teenager, a young adult, a lover, a parent, a worker, a grandparent and so on. Moving from one role to another involves change—some people cope very well and others flounder. For some of us, the thought of being a grandparent is beyond comprehension, 'surely I'm not that old', while for others it signals a wonderful milestone and the chance for us once again to share our lives with younger people.

- *Appearance*—we tend to lose our youthful 'good looks' and body shape as we get on in years. It can be rather devastating for some of us who see 'youthful' as okay and elderly as not okay. Wrinkles may appear, our hair begin to thin, our waistlines begin to thicken. We need to learn to cope with these changes adaptively if we are to feel okay about ourselves.

8

◆ *Physical abilities*—our ability to run as fast and jump as high as we were once able to declines as we get on in years. This is certainly not to say that we cannot keep ourselves extremely fit and active as we get older, however we do need to adapt to the change in our ability levels and begin to set personal goals for ourselves, rather than expect to compete with the more youthful. When we adapt to the changes in our physical abilities in this manner, we find that our *self-esteem* and *self-dignity* levels remain high and our wasted worry about getting older diminishes. Another important positive from adapting to these changes is that because we *feel good* about ourselves and still enjoy the challenges of life, we keep participating in life instead of withdrawing from it.

◆ *Others' opinions*—about you and your worth may alter as you begin to age. Employers may see you as being too old for a particular role in the organisation because they may feel that youth equals more enthusiasm, adaptation to change and energy. Your ability to cope with the change in others' perceptions is also vital so that your self-esteem does not become vulnerable or you do not become overly paranoid about what might happen to you, or how others are viewing you. You need to be able to make quick and effective changes if you find yourself in this sort of situation. This negative perception of the effects of ageing can also occur in your personal life when someone may feel you are 'over the hill'.

RELATIONSHIPS

There are many changes to various forms of our relationships that occur as we travel the road of life. As children, we have a dependent relationship with our parents; during the teenage years we begin to discover the trials and tribulations associated with becoming less dependent on our parents, and as adults most of us are quite independent. Interestingly, later in life our parents may become dependent on us for support and caring as they reach the twilight of their lives—a nice opportunity to repay the love and caring they hopefully showed you as a child. The more intimate relationships we develop as adults may also change. Spouses or partners may break up relationships leaving us to form new meaningful relationships with others. For many people these changes can be very difficult to deal with as they may involve leaving a 'comfort zone' that has various forms of security associated with it, including financial, emotional, lifestyle and so on. We may also find it affects the relationship we have with our children.

VOCATION AND WORK CHANGES

Once again there are many realms within our working environments that can pose an enormous amount of change; these include:

◆ *Changes in technology*—a constant source of frustration for many people is trying to keep abreast of the rampant changes that are occurring in this area. Computer software packages and hardware are updated so regularly, often before people report feeling on top of the last package. All forms of communication systems are changing rapidly requiring the people using and operating them to adapt or become overwhelmed by the pace and complexity of the changes. Learning to master it all can be quite challenging for many, but for others it evokes fear and anxiety.

◆ *Changes in work practices*—the way we go about our work also changes. We now have a great emphasis on teamwork with buzz words like 'empowerment', 'ownership', 'visions', 'missions', 'best practice', 'total quality management', 'multi-skilling' and so on. Re-organising is becoming a very common and dynamic practice with 'downsizing or rightsizing' being instituted on a wide scale, often resulting in fewer people doing more, and the need for a broader range of skills and the necessity to be able to cope with these types of changes quickly and on a fairly regular basis.

Various forms of systems and policies can also change regularly such as equal employment opportunity legislation and practices, anti-discrimination legislation, unfair dismissal legislation and enterprise bargaining. No doubt about it, the workplaces, both private and public, of the 1990s are very dynamic and ever-changing environments.

SOCIAL AND COMMUNITY CHANGES

Another area of fairly constant change, not always that obvious, involves aspects of our social and community activities. Social values and expectations have changed quite dramatically during the last few decades as have community values and systems. We now have laws to protect minority groups. It is now an offence to be discriminatory, and multiculturalism is certainly a well-entrenched facet of life.

Many nationalities are now sharing aspects of each other's cultural roots and co-existing in a way that a few decades ago would have been far more difficult. There are now many support programs and services to assist people in settling into what can be a vastly different social and community situation for them. People are having to adapt to the many changes of settling into a new culture, or accepting aspects of another culture into the established culture in their country of birth.

If we are not open to the new and novel aspects of other cultures, we may view these as an intrusion into a way of life that we were very content and happy with and so, feel rather bitter about what is being forced upon us. The changes to our lifestyle then, are a source of stress and frustration leading to a resistance against those changes.

WHY THE NEED FOR CHANGE?

We can avoid this question no longer! There is definitely a need for changes to occur both within us and in the world around us, the major reasons being:

PROGRESS

Medical research has assisted many people with all sorts of illnesses and disabilities, to have a far higher quality of life than they may have had several decades ago. We have been able to eradicate many of the rampant killer diseases of the past.

As well, transport, computers, facilities, systems of all types have generally improved and continue to improve so that people in many parts of the world, but by no means all, can go about their lives with more knowledge and certainty than in the past.

PURPOSE

A change in the way things are done adds a challenge and purpose to our lives. Human beings really do crave novelty in their lives. Without it we can quickly become demotivated and begin to 'rust out', with symptoms of lethargy, depression and low performance. When we do not have a 'meaningful pursuit' to follow, we tend to go into a void state for a period of time, with neither positive nor negative consequences.

However, if we stay in the void state long enough, we will tend to drift into negative and non-productive behaviour and attitudes.

This generally ends up with a 'why bother' attitude—'nothing good ever happens to me, it's everybody else who gets the lucky breaks in life'. A rather sad state of affairs, and unfortunately all too common.

NOVELTY

We know that humans need novelty in their lives. We need new and exciting adventures to look forward to, not necessarily major life events, but events with enough uncertainty and risk-taking to tingle the nerve endings from time to time. New experiences add a zest and vigour to life which assists us in remaining motivated and challenged rather than bored and lethargic. People who have novelty in their lives are generally far more interesting and positive to be around; they exude a certain energy and zest for life which is missing from those of us who only stick to the routine.

Change provides us with novelty. Even very minor changes may bring enough novelty to stimulate and enhance our sense of well being, the change most certainly does not have to be of major proportions.

CHALLENGE

Challenge provides us with both energy and purpose. Without challenges in life our problems can become both self-defeating and energy-zapping. When we perceive something as a challenge, the energy flows inward, we lean forward and think 'okay, how can I get on top of this thing?'. When we look on something in life as a problem, the energy tends to flow out of our bodies and we think 'this is too difficult, I can't stand it'. Change in our lives provides us with many challenges as long as we see the changes in this light, rather than seeing them as debilitating problems.

OUR OWN MARK

As human beings, we have a need to be special and make our own mark in life as we move through it. If we were not able to participate in, and at times implement and force change, life would lose much of its meaning and purpose for us. Many would find themselves in the 'what's it all about Alfie' syndrome.

It would be terribly difficult to remain motivated and energised in life if what we were involved in did not seem to be improving things for ourselves or others. Each generation tends to question what has been done before and how effective it has been. That generation then goes about working out new or 'better' ways of doing things and so changes occur and continue to occur as each new generation comes along.

So you can see that there are quite a few reasons why change is necessary and why we are stuck with it. There are certain periods of history when changes have occurred on a greater magnitude and at a faster pace. One such period was the Industrial Revolution, when much of the world moved from an agricultural base to an industrial base. In our own time, technological changes are occurring at a very rapid rate and are difficult for many people to keep pace with. These changes often impact on our work and personal lives and people attempt to cope in many different ways.

There are also many aspects of our social system that are changing in major ways. For example, in fairly recent times we have embraced legislation to promote equal employment opportunity and anti-discrimination practices for all; there has been major emphasis on women's issues; we have changed the language we use for many disadvantaged or handicapped people; and we have embarked on a multicultural crusade.

Put all these sorts of changes occurring in our world together with the changes that are occurring directly to all of us, and you have a rather dynamic process that can either enhance your quality of life or severely detract from it. The chapters to follow in this book will help you to adapt and make the most of the changes rather than become a *victim* to them.

Remember that at the end of the day it is up to you how you react to changes in your life, what ones you go with and what ones you reject. However, we do need to guard against reacting negatively to changes just because we become defensive or are frightened by them. If we do not consider the changes occurring around us in an objective and rational manner we may miss out on wonderful opportunities.

QUICK QUIZ

Do you think most changes happening around you lead to an improvement in quality of life for people?   Yes/No

When something changes in your life do you tend to see it as a problem or a challenge? Please circle one.   Problem/Challenge

Do you enjoy most of the challenges that are there in your life?   Yes/No

Do you look forward to new and novel things happening in your life?   Yes/No

If you have answered *Yes* to most of the above, and circled the word *Challenge,* then you are shaping up as someone who enjoys and probably reacts well to change. We will explore this further in the next few chapters!

Are there particular changes you want or need to make in your life?—for example:

Coping better with growing older?   Yes/No

Sorting out particular relationships?   Yes/No

Work issues that need resolving?   Yes/No

Change something in your social life?   Yes/No

Become a more positive person?   Yes/No

More/less involvement in community activities?   Yes/No

How are you feeling about making these changes?

_____

_____

_____

_____

_____

_____

SUMMARY

◆ Change is a necessary part of our lives! Although we cannot always control the changes we will face, we _can_ control the way we react to them.

◆ Change may be:
   − desired or undesired;
   − controllable or uncontrollable;
   − gradual or immediate;
   − useful or not useful;
   − large or small;
   − forced or voluntary.

◆ Our _resistance_ to changes in our lives often depends upon the _importance_ and _controllability_ of the particular changes.

◆ Common changes we face include:
   − the ageing process, which includes different roles and expectations, our appearance, physical abilities and others' opinions of us;
   − relationships;
   − vocation and work changes;
   − social and community changes.

◆ Why the need for change? What does change bring into our lives?
   − progress;
   − purpose in life;

 - novelty;

 - challenge;

 - an opportunity to make our own mark.

◆ Remember that it is up to you what changes you accept and reject. You need to consider all changes in an objective and rational manner.

◆ What did the quick quiz indicate to you about you and your attitude to change?

CHAPTER 3

How does change affect us?

Although there is a great variation in the way people react to changes occurring in their lives, there is a particular pattern of responses that occur on a frequent basis. Many people go through a number of *stages* as they try to cope with what has happened and what is happening. It is important to understand these stages and the emotions, attitudes and behaviours we may exhibit when going through a particular stage. This insight can help us work out whether we are adapting or maladapting to whatever is occurring. We can then modify our reactions or seek assistance to cope better.

Hugh Mackay who is a psychologist and social researcher, has compiled more than 60 reports on the attitudes and behaviour of Australians since 1979 and has written a book called *Reinventing Australia: The Mind and Mood of Australia in the 90s*. In it he states that,

> One of the things we know about human beings is that, in general, they are resistant to change. Even when there are small interruptions to the rhythm and pattern of daily life, most people experience mild tension or irritation. When our lives are disrupted by changes which involve some redefinition of who we are or how we are going to live, the tension is correspondingly greater.

Mackay argues that 'today's fear of the future is not so much based on what the future holds as on our inability to chart a confident course through it'—and I certainly agree with him, with the emphasis here on *confident*. According to Mackay, Australians in the last quarter of this century have become pioneers in that we have been plunged into a period of unprecedented social, cultural, economic, political and technological change which has caused the Australian way of life to be 'radically redefined'.

CASE STUDY

Andrew, a 34-year-old solicitor with a large insurance company, was on his way home from work. He had to pick up his two daughters from pre-school and was running late. Coming up to the last set of traffic lights before the kindergarten he noticed they had just turned amber so he speeded up hoping to get across the intersection. Just as he began to speed up, a car crossed lanes, pulled in front of him and stopped at the lights. Andrew lost control; he pulled up behind the car, got out of his car and began yelling abuse at the young female driver in the car. As the lights turned green he kicked the side panel of her car, as the young driver—hysterical by this time—sped away. Andrew returned to his car as other motorists began beeping him with their car horns.

As Andrew continued towards the child care centre and began to calm down, the full extent of what had happened began to dawn on him. He suddenly burst into tears not believing what he had done, and then a sense of panic also overcame him as he realised that other motorists would have recorded his number plate and he might be faced with trouble and embarrassment.

The reason Andrew was late and hurrying to pick up his daughters before the child care centre closed was that at a quarter to five he had been called into his director's office, informed that he had just been made redundant and that he had 30 minutes to gather his personal belongings and leave the premises escorted by a security guard. He could use the company's outplacement services!

So, are there recognised stages or patterns of coping with change that people go through when they are exposed to this myriad of changes during their lifetime?—let alone the hassles and traumas of everyday living which may have nothing at all to do with these more major societal changes. There are four major stages which people can move through, as the diagram below illustrates.

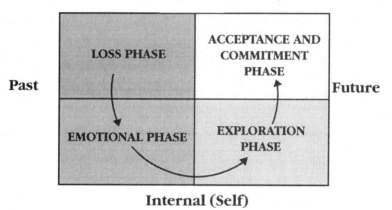

STAGES OF CHANGE

FIRST STAGE—LOSS PHASE

When a major or significant change occurs in our lives, our first reaction is likely to be one of denial or what is quite commonly referred to as 'shock'. It is almost as if the brain is trying to protect us by not absorbing the full impact of what is happening all at once, but preparing us to cope by allowing us to gradually come to grips with what has happened or is happening. If we are well prepared for a particular change which is to occur in life then we may go through this stage early on, when we first hear about the change, rather than later on when the event or change actually happens.

The signs and symptoms of being in this phase or stage of change include withdrawal, a focus on the past, a sense of numbing, depersonalisation—a rather strange phenomenon of not really being with yourself, purposeless behaviour or a lot of activity with very little being achieved. You may also experience a dulling of your emotions and feel that you ought to be more upset than you actually are. A phenomenon known as *bargaining* can also occur during this initial stage. This is characterised by the person making all sorts of 'bargains' or promises if the events involved in the change do not occur, or if events can be retracted. Even though the person doing the bargaining may consider it to be irrational he or she tends to be driven on by panic.

This initial loss phase can last for varying periods of time depending on what has happened and how it has been communicated to you. It can last anything from two hours to five days.

There is a very common tendency to concentrate on the past with thoughts and attitudes like:

- ◆ wasn't it great when . . .;
- ◆ if only we could turn back time;
- ◆ they were the good old days;
- ◆ those times will never return.

CASE STUDY

Vicki had been going out with her boyfriend for 18 months and thought that they would probably become engaged before the end of the year. He rang her on Friday to say he could not go out to dinner with friends on the Saturday night as they had organised, but that he would call her Sunday to explain. On Sunday morning he rang to say that he no longer wished to go out with her and that he was returning the clothes she had left at his place. He hung up before Vicki could ask him why he did not want to see her any more.

Vicki was stunned—she did not cry or become hysterical but felt a rather strange numbing experience. She went about her day catching up with friends for coffee and having dinner with her family.

Strangely enough that night she dropped off to sleep quickly but woke at 1.30 a.m. feeling quite panicky and overwhelmed. She could not get back to sleep. Vicki's mind was racing with thoughts of how life would be impossible without him, maybe it was all just a bad dream, maybe he was confused and did not mean what he had said. She was looking for something to hold on to that would restore things to the way they had been before the phone call. It was the way she wanted things to be.

SECOND STAGE—EMOTIONAL PHASE

Following the initial stage we then move into a stage characterised by heightened emotional responses and a very real resistance to accepting the change or changes.

The most common *sign and symptom* in this stage is anger. The anger may go outwards in terms of blaming others or inwards in terms of blaming ourselves for what is happening. There are generally varying degrees of anxiety experienced, ranging from fleeting bouts to major panic attacks. Depression is commonly associated with this phase, and like anxiety, can be experienced in varying degrees. Resentment regarding the change is also usually high and we may actually try to sabotage what is happening. During this stage people may actually act in ways which are completely out of character. When we look back on what we may have done during this time we often feel a sense of disbelief and guilt.

CASE STUDY

Steve's second marriage, to Judy had lasted seven years. They had experienced a rather stormy relationship which ended when

Judy informed Steve she was leaving him to live with her boss, who was also leaving his wife. The night that Judy informed him of her intentions, Steve took an overdose of medication which led to him spending five days in hospital. Judy felt so guilty about Steve's attempted suicide that she moved back home and told Steve she would give the relationship another chance.

Why do we resist change, find it so threatening and become so emotional about it? There are obviously many reasons, but generally they can be placed under a few headings, which include:

◆ *exhaustion*—we can become worn out by change when the change goes on for some time, or we experience a number of changes in a relatively short period of time;

◆ *comfort zone*—we become used to doing things a certain way and we feel in control and comfortable because we feel we know what is expected of us and get into a routine with our lives;

◆ *lack of control*—it is difficult to support things when we feel they are very much out of our control and that we will have little influence in where they go or how they get there;

◆ *fear*—the unknown! It is quite common for people to develop the 'what if …' syndrome. 'What if things don't work out well?' 'What if I find it difficult to keep up?' or worse still, 'what if I find it impossible to learn the new skills?', or 'what if I can't cope by myself?'

If we only allow these reasons to interfere with our well-being for a short period of time, then not much damage is likely to occur. However if we get trapped in any one of the above scenarios for an extended period of time then we may well end up maladapting to the change or changes occurring in our life.

Later in the book I will show you how to 'break out' of any of these unhealthy resistance habits you may have developed.

THIRD STAGE—EXPLORATION PHASE

You know you have reached this stage when you begin to experiment and participate in the new way of doing things or with a new lifestyle. You will not feel totally at ease and may still feel quite apprehensive about certain things; however you begin to accept that this is the way it is going to be and perhaps you can survive the change and make a go of it after all. A person is sometimes described as being in this stage when the 'driving forces' towards becoming involved in the change take over from the 'restraining forces', that is, when the person begins to focus on the positives ahead rather than the positives of the past.

While in this stage and becoming focused on participating in what is happening, a person can also regress to the emotional phase if something does not go their way or doesn't go that well. Hopefully what happens however, is that the person develops an *attraction* to the new things he or she is involved in and gradually moves into the fourth stage.

CASE STUDY

Richard and Erica had been married for 17 years. When Richard died suddenly of a heart attack, Erica felt devastated. She spent most of her time at home by herself and occasionally visited her daughter. Friends had become frustrated at the constant refusals by Erica to meet them for coffee or to join them for a meal.

One day a close friend, John, visited Erica and shared his own experiences following the death of his wife Vanessa after a long battle with cancer. He explained how he had virtually hibernated for 18 months following his wife's death until he asked himself what his wife would want him to do, and realised she would want him to make the most of his life. John explained that he began to phone friends again and go out socially, and while he continued to miss Vanessa he was able to focus more and more on the good times they shared during their life, and enjoy his new lifestyle without her.

Erica decided to follow John's advice. She is gradually rebuilding a new life without Richard and is beginning to enjoy her life again. There are still times when she becomes quite depressed. However, these are becoming infrequent and do not last as long.

FOURTH STAGE—ACCEPTANCE AND COMMITMENT

This stage is characterised by the formation of new habits and a commitment towards making a success of the change in your life. It is a time of renewed energy and motivation leading to new achievements and accomplishments. The past is now tucked fairly firmly away in the memory and only looks appealing if you come under unusual amounts of stress in your life. Under those circumstances people can find themselves longing for the 'old ways' again. This is generally a time of embracing the change and making longer term plans which the person would have found difficult in any of the other stages. A sense of purpose and enthusiasm returns as people begin to look for new challenges in their personal or work lives.

When a person has accepted change, he or she begins to talk and act in a far more optimistic manner. The future begins to look rosy and a belief that life is worthwhile returns. Perhaps the simplest way to explain this stage is that life has returned to a state of normality, maybe even better than a previous normality, with the opportunity to enjoy new and novel experiences.

CASE STUDY

Maria was shocked when her partner of three years walked out on her saying that he had had a homosexual lover for the past 12 months. Initially she could not believe it and felt that he was confused and would work through the situation with her. When it became clear that he was not coming back, Maria became extremely angry and embarrassed at what had happened.

She moved to a new suburb and saw little of her friends and family. When a work mate called to see her late on a Saturday morning, she was still in bed recovering from a binge drinking episode the night before. Her work mate refused to leave, insisted Maria have a shower, get dressed and have lunch with her at the local café. Although she did not eat much, Maria listened as her friend explained how she had allowed herself to become a victim because of what had happened and that she needed to take some 'ownership' of her life; realise that what had occurred was a pain, not a major catastrophe and that she needed to take control of her life back.

Maria sat there, feeling angry and sorry for herself. When she got home that afternoon Maria began to feel mildly excited as if a heavy weight was released from around her shoulders— her friend from work had been right! She decided that she was no longer going to act out a victim role. She rang two friends whom she had not seen for some time and arranged to go to a movie with them that evening.

From that time on Maria looked for every opportunity she could find to socialise with friends; she arranged weekends away, and began playing netball again. Three months later she met Paul and has been seeing him now for eight months. Maria is also planning a two-month trip through Europe at the end of the year.

THE STAGES—HOW DOES IT ALL WORK?

One of the most common questions asked about the stages is 'do people move through them in that exact order and do all people react the same?' The answer is of course, *no*. Everybody reacts slightly differently to the same type of change occurring in their lives and everybody will move through the stages differently.

People spend different amounts of time in each stage and some people will actually jump one or two stages. Others appear to be working through the stages in a fairly standard way and something will happen in their lives which sees them regress a stage.

How people react to changes in their lives depends a great deal on their past experiences and present circumstances. If you have experienced significant changes and life events in the past, you coped well with them and they turned out okay, then you may be a little unnerved by a recent happening but will probably move quickly to the acceptance stage and find appropriate solutions to what is happening. If, on the other hand, you have not coped well with changes in your life and dread certain events occurring, it is likely you will spend quite some time in the emotional and assimilation phases when those changes occur. You may find it difficult to get to the acceptance and commitment stage.

Present circumstances also play a role in coping with change. Sometimes we can get firmly entrenched in a comfort zone where we feel secure and in control of our environment. If something threatens this zone we can panic and become quite emotional. The other scenario that will affect present coping abilities will be the amount of *stressors* we are exposed to at that time—the more stressors, the more unlikely it is that we will adjust well to the changes, as our coping resources get worn away by the demands placed on us. It is as though our 'adaptation energy' has been used up coping with the other situations in our life.

It is not only individuals who can go through these stages of adapting to change: families and staff teams can also experience these reactions if something happens which directly affects more than one person. For example, the notification that your company has been taken over by a competitor and the future of the company and it's employees is uncertain, can be enough to throw complete staff teams into the loss or shock stage, followed by many moving into the emotional stage when the redundancies are announced. Some staff may see the redundancies as an opportunity to pay off their mortgage and semi-retire, and these people will move straight to the acceptance stage. So you may in fact have employees in different stages at different times following a particular change, depending largely on the impact the individual employee perceives the change will have on him or her.

Families can also experience a very similar thing. For example the loss of a house due to fire may leave the husband in shock, while the wife sees it as a great opportunity to use the insurance money to buy a brand new house in a different suburb.

The next chapter is very interesting as it will assist you to work out how prepared you are for change in your life.

SUMMARY

◆ There are four common stages people go through when adapting to change.

- first stage—loss phase;

- second stage—emotional phase;

- third stage—exploration phase;

- fourth stage—acceptance and commitment.

◆ There is great variation in the way people react to change.

◆ People move through the stages quite differently.

◆ It is common for people to begin adapting and then regress due to specific life events.

CHAPTER 4

Are you ready for change? The five stages of readiness

It is all very well to talk about the benefits of adapting to change that occurs in our life, and let's face it, many changes are out of our control and if we are going to have a happy and rewarding future we need to accept what has happened and rebuild a new life. Why do so many of us have trouble doing this, accepting that change has occurred or will occur and making the most of it? It is because there are stages of readiness for change.

Understanding where we are in terms of our readiness for change is extremely important as it is a direct indicator for what we need to do in order to move to the next stage. The stages of readiness are linked to the stages of change which were talked about in the last chapter, and I will explain the linkage as we go.

STAGES OF READINESS

PRE-CONTEMPLATION

1 In this stage we are quite happy doing what we are doing and feel that generally everything is well in the world. Even though what we are doing may be maladaptive, we are not aware that it is, so we continue living in our comfort zone. We may be quite shocked if anyone points out that we have not adapted well to the change or changes and that we need to look at doing things differently. You can become quite defensive at this time, attempting to rationalise your attitudes and behaviours or attempting to throw the burden back on the other person—accusing that person of being naive or lacking in understanding.

CONTEMPLATION

2 This stage of readiness for change is the next step in deciding to do something more constructive regarding the change. It is a stage characterised by uncertainty and ambivalence. We may not be sure we are capable of adapting better or doing things differently and, of course, we may not be sure that we want to. There may have been some payoffs in reacting the way we were, such as feeling sorry for ourselves or being able to justify the anger we were displaying. However, in this stage we begin to entertain the idea of a better way—'maybe life would be more fulfilling if I started going out more' or 'perhaps the redundancy has created the opportunity for me to consider other career options—this may not be as awful as I thought!', and so on.

During this stage our attitudes will dart back and forth between attempting to do things differently or remaining on the same path. This stage involves a lot of analysis, but generally little action.

PREPARATION

3 At this stage the balance has tipped in favour of doing something different to try to cope more effectively. This stage is characterised by more action than the previous stage of uncertainty and ambivalence. Now the person actually prepares for change believing that there will indeed be benefits from the change. Even before any new strategies are implemented, some old habits may be dropped or altered.

ACTION

4 There is now a definite strategy in place for the change to occur. Significant people may have been contacted or involved in determining the strategy. There is now a plan of action and we begin to invoke that action and determine the cost benefit analysis. What is the cost to us in changing and doing things differently? What are the benefits? This is not always an easy stage to remain in and it is common for people to regress to an earlier stage.

MAINTENANCE

5 Effort now needs to be applied to maintaining and consolidating the changes. Some of us will be successful on the first attempt at implementing any changes in our lives. For others it will take a number of attempts. Maintenance of any change is really all about how we *focus* and *direct* our *energy*. If we remain focused on the new tasks at hand and put a good deal of energy into these, we will—in most cases—be extremely successful, and we may even generalise the benefits of the change into other aspects of our lives. We may use the opportunity to re-evaluate what we are doing in life and what our goals really are. Other changes may therefore result.

Some people require little assistance in successfully moving from a state of pre-contemplation to maintaining their action plan once they have decided on it. Others will require a range of assistance, from support from friends or loved ones through to professional counselling and coaching. The main thing here is that no matter what support you feel you need, you feel okay about getting it. After all, it is your life and you are the only one who can live it. It is important that you maximise the quality of your life and at times this may mean that you have to admit that you need a hand in coping with particular events or situations that are affecting you. Remember that if you do this you may one day be in a position to pass the knowledge and experience you have gained onto someone else.

READINESS FOR CHANGE QUIZ

Please circle *yes* or *no* depending on how you feel about the question.

I expect things to be the way they are now forever.	Yes/No
Things will work out okay no matter what I do.	Yes/No
Why bother changing, things always return to normal.	Yes/No
The old ways are always the best ways.	Yes/No
I'm too old to change my ways.	Yes/No
Even when I start new things I never stick to them.	Yes/No
That's just the way I am and I will always be that way.	Yes/No
I don't need to change; I'm quite happy, thank you.	Yes/No
The effort in changing is just not worthwhile.	Yes/No
I am incapable of doing things differently.	Yes/No

SCORING

Yes—If you have circled five or more you are really not ready for major changes in your life. You probably do need to seek assistance in coming to terms with what is happening in your life.

No—If you have circled five or more you are certainly on your way to adapting to the necessary changes in your life. Keep at it and seek whatever help you feel you need. The rest of the book will certainly assist you in doing this, and if necessary seek professional assistance.

SUMMARY

◆ There are five stages of readiness for change:
- Pre-contemplation
- Contemplation
- Preparation
- Action
- Maintenance.
◆ Readiness for change quiz—how did you fare?

CHAPTER 5

Preparing for changes in life

How do you prepare to cope with the many challenges life will undoubtedly throw your way? Is it possible? I mean, how the dickens can you prepare when you don't know when or where many of the changes will come from and what form they might take when they do come? In all reality do you just have to sit back and cope the best you can when it is all happening  around you? Well no, you don't! You certainly can prepare, and in doing so, buffer yourself against many of the normal stresses of unexpected or unwanted change, and even change that is sought, such as getting married or the birth of a child.

In preparing ourselves for changes in life it is essential that we make sure we develop an *ownership* mentality towards whatever has happened, or is about to happen. The reverse of this situation is a *victim* mentality. When we are in a *victim* role we blame others for why life is not the way we would like it to be, or perhaps blame ourselves that we are hopeless and useless and unable to cope with change at all.

THE OWNERSHIP ROLE

The *ownership* role is one where we have an attitude that basically says 'if it's to be it's up to me'. You take responsibility for your reaction to what is happening in life, whether you brought it on yourself or not. It is the realisation that no matter what events take place in life, we need to be able to deal with them effectively and not seek or make excuses as to why things are not working out the way we would like them to.

Here's a tip—life does not come with an iron clad guarantee that things will always be the way we would like them to be and that we will not have to deal with disruptions and events that are a pain in the butt. The only guarantee is that things will not always go our way!

THE VICTIM ROLE

What is a victim role and what are the characteristics of it? We need to be aware of it, or at least work out if at this point in our lives we have fallen into it. The following diagram explains how it all works. The victim role is generally recognised by the concept of *external control*.

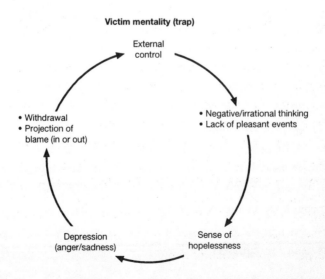

By external control, I am referring to that process by which we blame outside factors for our high stress levels regarding what is happening, and so, we believe that there is really nothing that we can do about it.

As the diagram on the previous page shows, if we develop a mentality (attitudes and beliefs) which says that everything else is to blame for our stress and inability to cope, we tend to become very negative and irrational in our thinking.

We say and think things like 'it gets me upset', 'I can't stand it', 'they should do the right thing by me', 'nothing ever works out right for me'.   Now, let's consider these little snippets one at a time. Later in the book I will go into more detail about irrational thinking and what you can do about it if you recognise that you are doing it.

♦ *'it gets me upset'*—let's rethink this one. Nobody gets you upset; you get yourself upset by what you say to yourself about what has happened. We often make mountains out of molehills by telling ourselves that something is terrible and a major catastrophe when it is generally merely an inconvenience and unlikely to be life-threatening. You can get yourself very upset if you allow this negative 'self-talk' and attitude to continue.

♦ *'I can't stand it'*—of course you can stand it! The only reason you are having trouble standing it is because you are telling yourself exactly that, and how 'terrible' and 'awful' it is. Keep it in perspective. Try saying 'it is not what I wanted to happen, I feel upset, so what can I do about it to resolve it as well as possible?'.

♦ *'they should do the right thing by me'*—it would be nice if they did the 'right thing' by you, but they have not! Remember there is no universal law saying they cannot do this and they will certainly not get locked up for it. You have choices—you can:

– approach them nicely and try to resolve it;

– accept it has happened and work out the most positive course of action for yourself;

– use it as an opportunity to change your lifestyle and do
something different;

– take them off your guest list!

◆ *'nothing ever works out right for me'*—here we go again using
what psychologists refer to as 'over-generalisations'. Of course
things 'work out' for you, they just may not have this time! Just
reflect for a minute on all the times that things have gone well
for you and you will realise that you have over-exaggerated,
possibly by a mile. We look at what others haven't done for us
and forget about what they *have* done; we also look at what we
haven't done or can't do and forget about what we *have* done and
what we *can* do.

This is a common knee-jerk reaction which many of us can
get into if we are not careful, and we then allow ourselves to fall
into the victim trap.

Now when our thinking, attitudes and beliefs become all
negative and irrational, we obviously lose the ability to enjoy
what is happening in life, so there seems to be a shortage of
pleasant events. This is not because the events are not there,
but because we have lost the ability to see them in a positive
and invigorating manner. This situation can then lead to us
feeling a sense of hopelessness about our ability to cope and
regain control over our lives, because we believe it is others or
other things that cause our distress and control our happiness.
This sense of hopelessness can then lead to those symptoms of
panic such as depression, anger, anxiety, fear or sadness.

These symptoms can then see us project even more blame out or in, and because we are depressed and cynical we often tend to withdraw from people, situations and sometimes life in general. You need to remain aware that not preparing to cope with changes in life could have major ramifications across many areas of your life.

This whole scenario only serves to reinforce that you have no control over the changes that occur or are likely to occur in your life, and the nasty symptoms you feel as a result. You then tend to get caught in the 'trap' and go round and round the spiral of change as indicated before.

So what can you do? Well, you need to break out of the victim role and the victim trap and head into the *owner mentality* by developing more internal control. When we do this, we tend to involve ourselves in the ownership cycle, which is a far more positive spiral to be in, enabling us to foster the types of attitudes, beliefs and behaviours that keep us there. The diagram on page 39 explains what happens when we make the transition to the ownership role when dealing with changes in life.

When you make the journey to the *ownership role* or if you are already in it, you develop a good solid sense of internal control. Internal control is happening when you take responsibility for running your life and effectively managing whatever those changes are and whatever happens along the way, including any potential stressors or sources of distress. We develop an attitude which says 'if it's to be, it's up to me'. We can certainly seek guidance and reassurance from others, but what we don't do is 'spit the dummy' when things don't go our way.

We acknowledge that it is not the way we would have liked it to be, and try to work out what is the best thing we can do about it right now. In other words we go into solution mode and look for a resolution to whatever is happening.

Whenever we do this, we use positive and adaptive thinking, and rational behavioural and emotional reactions. It helps us

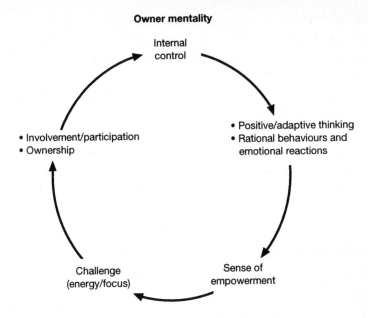

Owner mentality

Internal control

• Positive/adaptive thinking
• Rational behaviours and emotional reactions

Sense of empowerment

Challenge (energy/focus)

• Involvement/participation
• Ownership

to keep things in perspective and to remain flexible, positive and solution-orientated in the way we go about living our lives, especially when we interact with others. When we go about our life in this manner, we develop a sense of empowerment where we realise that we can control our reactions to changes in our lives and keep our distress levels under control.

This is an extremely positive approach and we need to practise it at every opportunity in life, so that we really build up those skills for preparing for any sort of change in our lives. When we develop the ownership skills we see situations in life as a challenge, where our energy and focus go into positive, purposeful behaviour and attitudes to resolve and achieve things in the best possible manner.

Once you have begun this journey, you accept the ownership role and you use *involvement* and *participation* with people or in situations, to achieve those goals in life which are important to you. Expected or unexpected changes are then used to your best advantage rather than seen as a major hurdle or stumbling block. This serves to reinforce your sense of internal control over your reactions to whatever happens in your life, and that you can and do make a difference to the quality of your life through all sorts of changes. You then spiral around in the ownership role taking more and more control over your destiny and achieving the things many others only dream of. You will also do it in a manner which lessens the stresses on you for most of the journey through life.

At the end of the day the choice is yours—*victim* or *owner*. This book will show you how to develop the owner role—a role I sincerely recommend.

CHANGE AND POSSIBLE SOLUTIONS

To help you further understand that you can control your levels of perceived anxiety regarding changes in life, I will now introduce you to a way of thinking about and categorising any event, change or situation in your life. How you deal with any change will depend on which category it falls into. You can place any change that happens in life into one of these four categories.

The change is either:

◆ important and controllable;

◆ important and uncontrollable;

◆ unimportant and controllable; or

◆ unimportant and uncontrollable.

Once you have placed the change into the appropriate category in terms of how you view it, then there are four possible solutions or sets of skills for managing the change.

You may use:

◆ awareness skills;

◆ acceptance skills;

◆ coping skills; or

◆ action skills.

Now, these possible solutions are interesting. Sometimes just being aware of what the effect of change can be upon you, or to understand why you are getting uptight, is enough to have you turn the stress or resistance of change to a short-lived minor irritation. Sometimes, however, you need to accept that what is happening or what has happened was out of your control, so you may need to change your attitude towards it and what you are realistically able to do about it.

At other times coping may be the best solution. This is where you are able to change or develop your behaviours, beliefs and emotional responses to the situation. This allows you to cope with the changes better. Then of course, there are the situations where you need to go into some form of action mode to cope with and resolve whatever that particular change may be. You may need to interact differently with someone or something, or cope better with new circumstances in your environment.

Let's now have a look at a few examples of changes in life, putting situations and possible solutions together.

IMPORTANT AND CONTROLLABLE

Consider the following example. Your boss tells you that there is a manager's position available in another department in the company and he is offering you the job. Your boss explains that you do not have to accept it, however, he feels it would be in your own best interest to do so. You certainly have wanted to move to a higher position in the company, however you have negative feelings about the team in that area and especially about the person you would be reporting to.

Solutions—you need to use your *awareness skills* to assist you in making the decision about the job. You may already have enough information to make a deliberate decision, or you may need to pursue it further. In making a decision you need to consider whether using *coping skills* would help you to deal with the negative things you had heard about, or decide not to take the job and wait for another opportunity.

IMPORTANT AND UNCONTROLLABLE

You have just been informed by your manager that your department is being restructured and that you have been made redundant. The redundancy package is quite generous so you have a good financial buffer to get you through for quite some time. The company has also organised an outplacement company to assist you in preparing yourself for, and acquiring another job. Initially your reaction was one of disbelief. This gradually turned to a mixture of anxiety and anger.

Solutions—You need to use *acceptance skills* to acknowledge that these sorts of things can happen in life. They certainly are a pain in the butt, but there is no universal law that states fairness and good fortune has to always come your way. You then need to make sure you are using effective *coping skills* and the positive *action skills* to deal as constructively as you possibly can with the situation at hand.

UNIMPORTANT AND CONTROLLABLE

You are beginning to feel quite frustrated and embarrassed by the state your lounge suite is in. You have been wondering what you can do about it.

Solutions—It certainly sounds like some 'change' is needed here. Your *awareness* is fine, realising that the lounge suite is

no longer a source of joy or comfort in your life, so using *coping skills* to try to put up with it is probably not a good idea especially if you have already been putting up with it for some time. You really do need to use *action skills* and do something about it such as sell it and buy another one, or perhaps recover it with a nice bright new fabric.

UNIMPORTANT AND UNCONTROLLABLE

Your teenage son gets an extremely 'modern' haircut that you do not like. Well it certainly is a change, however hardly world-shattering or a catastrophe in its own right.

Solutions—the most important skill to use here is *acceptance*. If it is not very important and something you cannot control, it is probably sensible to say nicely what you think of the cut and then get on with your life leaving your son's up to him. If you find you are getting angry and upset you will probably also need to use some *coping skills* involving a more rational attitude and remaining relaxed when you see your son. This assists in keeping your emotions under control because if your emotions become irrational and over the top, your attitudes and thinking will remain very negative and your behaviour will run amok on you as well—not a pleasant sight! Remember to keep it in perspective.

When I talk about something being *important* or *unimportant*, it is for you to decide where a particular change sits for you, remembering to keep it in perspective and not inadvertently make mountains out of molehills. The following exercise will identify your perception as to where the changes in your life fit.

Controllable or *uncontrollable* refers to the degree of say we have, or the part we play, in the changes occurring or coming about.

We certainly cannot control some changes occurring in our lives. We can however *control our reactions to them*. So when you do this next exercise I would like you to think about controllability—can you stop it happening or not? Don't consider it in terms of being able to control your reaction to it or not, because, as the rest of the book will point out, you can of course control your reaction to it.

This exercise involves thinking about changes occurring in your life in recent times, and placing them in one of the four categories below. See how you do!

Important and controllable   Important and uncontrollable

_____   _____

_____   _____

_____   _____

_____   _____

Unimportant and controllable   Unimportant and uncontrollable

_____   _____

_____   _____

_____   _____

_____   _____

Now come up with positive solutions you need to use to resolve or best deal with these changes that have occurred, are occurring, or may occur in your life. While this may still prove a somewhat difficult task at this stage, it still is a very useful exercise and you will probably surprise yourself!

'I feel the changes I have placed into the above categories would be best dealt with by using' (place each particular change noted under a possible solution):

Awareness   Acceptance   Coping   Action

_____   _____   _____   _____

_____   _____   _____   _____

_____   _____   _____   _____

_____   _____   _____   _____

As you go through this exercise you will gain an understanding that you *can* prepare for and that you *can* control your reaction to the changes that have, are, or may occur in your life. This means you also keep the potential stresses from those changes to a bare minimum. Remember that the idea is to have enough stimulation and pressure in life without the debilitating effects of too much ongoing stress.

SUMMARY

♦ An ownership mentality rather than a victim mentality regarding change is critical.

♦ Beware the victim trap.

♦ Four categories that events in life (change) can fall into:
- important and controllable;
- important and uncontrollable;
- unimportant and controllable;
- unimportant and uncontrollable.

♦ The four sets of skills for managing change are:
- awareness;
- acceptance;
- coping;
- action.

CHAPTER 6

Coping effectively with change

For many of us, comfort zones are important for our sense of emotional well-being. When something challenges or threatens our comfort zone or zones we can begin to feel, think and behave in ways that may certainly not be characteristic. Coping effectively with any change in our lives whether personal or work-related, is certainly possible and every day we see and hear of people adjusting wonderfully to all sorts of minor and major situations that have occurred or are occurring in their lives. To be able to do this successfully, we need to initiate effective *emotional*, *attitudinal* and *behavioural* control over ourselves as we go through the decision-making and problem-solving stages that will lead to the rebuilding of our lifestyle. By this I mean:

♦ *emotional*—feelings such as anxiety, fear, anger, resentment and guilt which will have a marked impact on our coping strategies;

- *attitudinal*—thoughts or 'self-talk' which will impact heavily on both our emotional state and our actions or behaviours; and

- *behavioural*—actions which we use to try to cope with what is happening, including trying to deal with the emotional and attitudinal ramifications of what is happening.

These three aspects of our being, which incidentally are the only things we are ever doing at any one time in our lives, are interrelated to the point where they will affect each other, so that the way we *feel* will affect the way we *think* and also the way we *act* or behave. The way we behave will also affect the way we think and our emotions and so on. So, if we allow any aspect to run astray, the effect on the other aspects could mean that we really do maladapt to any of those changes in our lives.

This chapter will draw our attention to what we can do to ensure that our emotions, attitude and behaviour remain flexible, adaptable, rational, positive and solution-orientated no matter what has happened, is happening, or may happen in our lives.

Now, as you consider the above, you also need to be aware of the general guide for surviving and benefiting from changes in life. This guide can be remembered as the *3R rule*. Following any major change you need to:

- *Recover*—regain your sense of balance and routine. Make time for yourself to do things you enjoy.

- *Refocus*—gain a realistic perspective on life by focusing on the 'big picture'. What possibilities are there in your life, what have you done and what can you do well? What are the opportunities and options open to you?

- *Regenerate*—get adequate rest, avoid alcohol and eat properly. Increase your circle of support and involve yourself in vocational, intimate, social and recreational pursuits.

This chapter also incorporates advice and techniques to ensure that you do *recover*, *refocus* and *regenerate* from any changes in your life. This will only occur if you master and control your emotions, attitudes and behaviours.

EFFECTIVE COPING

The major aspect of dealing with any changes in life is to develop an attraction to change, rather than a resistance to it. To develop an attraction to change, just like to any other thing in life, we need to focus on the stimulation, opportunity and growth that change can offer us, rather than remain paralysed by anxiety, fear or self-generated emotional trauma.

EMOTIONAL MATURITY

Being able to develop astute and rational coping skills requires a healthy amount of *emotional maturity*. By *emotional maturity* I mean the ability to *feel* whilst at the same time having *rational* and *positive thoughts* and *constructive actions*. Many of us have trouble coordinating these three things at the one time!

It appears that when certain emotions are felt, our rational thinking and smart behaviour goes out the window.

Certain changes in life can indeed be rather difficult to deal with emotionally. However, making the situation worse by allowing our emotions to govern how we run our lives is generally not the most astute way to go.

When we allow ourselves to run on raw emotions of anxiety or fear, our thinking can become very negative and irrational and we begin to say things to ourselves like 'this is terrible', 'I can't stand it', 'how will I ever cope?', 'this shouldn't happen to me, they must look after me', and then of course our emotions spiral even more out of control and before we know it we can end up in that victim trap.

CASE STUDY

Barbara was a 42-year-old mother of two young children who separated from her husband some 18 months previously.

She was working as a personal assistant in a large financial company when she and her boss were retrenched.

Barbara panicked and began thinking about the ramifications for her young family wondering how they would make ends meet. She began to imagine herself and the children living on the street and the welfare taking her children from her. Barbara began drinking quite heavily and only began getting herself together when her mother realised something was wrong and came to stay with her.

As part of the redundancy Barbara was able to use an outplacement firm to assist her in preparing to find another job. She approached one employment agency and began applying for jobs in the paper. Even before Barbara actually left her old job she had two new job offers—one from the agency and another through the paper. She was able to reflect on how unnecessary the heightened emotional state and negative attitudes had been.

Here's a tip—keep a handle on your emotions. Yes, many of the changes that take place in our lives may not be the ones that we would choose to happen. However we need to keep in mind that life does not come with any guarantees. We do not adapt better to crisis or change in our lives by reacting with emotional irrationality to these events. We cope effectively by using good problem-solving and decision-making techniques and bringing our emotional responses back under our control as soon as is possible.

THE EMOTIONAL MATURITY TEST

How *emotionally mature* are you, especially in your reactions to change in your life? How do you know if you have the *emotional maturity* to cope effectively with present or future changes that may occur in your life? The test you can take in a moment will alert you to your strengths or work areas (attitudes or beliefs you need to do something about) but let's first consider what emotional maturity is all about.

Definition—emotional maturity is measured by your ability to remain calm, positively focused and solution-orientated no matter what is happening in your life.

It is probably more important in terms of your overall well-being and possible achievements in life than your IQ level or what is considered to be your intellectual ability. Much effort has been put into improving our knowledge, skill and *intellectual maturity*; however very little attention or effort has gone into teaching people how to develop e*motional maturity*. So, how do we know what level of e*motional maturity* we have? It is about time to take the test.

Please answer the following questions as accurately and as honestly as you can. Remember, the profile obtained here is not for you or others to judge you by, but for you to use as a guide to self-improvement and self-growth.

Answer the following statements by choosing the one which is most like you and then circling the appropriate number:

very much like me	3
somewhat like me	2
maybe, maybe not	1
no, not at all like me	0

When I get angry I can quickly get myself back under control.

3   2   1   0

I cause and am responsible for the times I get irritable and moody.

3   2   1   0

I am aware of and can control my anxieties, fears and panic.

3   2   1   0

When things begin to overwhelm me I get my act together quickly.

3   2   1   0

I generally say what I think and do not bottle things up.

3   2   1   0

I am responsible for my own feelings; others cannot get me upset unless I let them.

3   2   1   0

I feel good about who I am and what I can achieve in life.

3   2   1   0

I believe I am certainly important to look after and do things for.

3   2   1   0

I do not let others' criticism of me affect me for long.

3   2   1   0

If I feel down or anxious I know I can get over it by being positive and solution-focused.

3   2   1   0

YOUR SCORE AND PROFILE

30–25: You have a very healthy level of emotional maturity and, from that aspect, a good chance of making the most of any changes that may come upon you in your journey through life.

24–15: Borderline! You are really in no person's land. Sometimes you may do okay and at other times not so okay. You need to make sure you read the rest of the book to gain more emotional maturity—which you certainly will if you practise the techniques and ideas put forward here. Reading about them is not enough. You must *practise, practise, practise*.

14-0: The lower your score in this section the more emphasis you need to place on developing a healthy level of emotional maturity. If you have trouble doing it by yourself, there is a chapter later in the book which tells you where you can get additional—and if need be—professional help and assistance.

Good on you for completing this profile. Do not judge yourself by it but use it as a catalyst and guide to change by if you need to. You can do it!

FOCUSING FOR EMOTIONAL CONTROL

One of the classic things that happens when our emotions begin to turn on us and start destroying our quality of life is that we start to lose the ability to focus on the positives and the strengths in our life. Instead we tend to use filtered thinking and focus on how terrible things are or will be, and perhaps on how terrible and hopeless we are, and we spiral into a depressive disorder, anxiety disorder or helplessness trap.

A psychological technique that assists greatly with controlling emotional reactions to events in life is one called *focusing*. It is a technique aimed at assisting us to get things back in perspective, to stop any worry habit that may have set in and to help in re-establishing our self-esteem.

When certain changes happen in life we can fill ourselves up with guilt and self-blame, destroy our own self-esteem, lose our confidence and begin to worry about everything and anything. We forget about all the things in life that we can do, the nice things about us and the coping capabilities we do have. Many of you will probably only need to read about this technique to gain some awareness, or to establish that you are already on the right track. Others will need to practise focusing on a fairly regular basis.

You would have already gained a fairly good idea of what focusing is all about. It requires us to concentrate on, and think about, all those things—small and large—that we do well throughout our normal day and during our journey through life. So let's get the negative focus out of the way. First up, we need to do this next exercise so we can more easily detect when our focus has become distorted towards the negatives. Use the exercise to list as many of your negative focuses as you can, especially those regarding a change or expected change in your life. List the things about this change that you worry about and focus on. Include any negative focuses you may also have regarding any future change you may feel will or could happen.

My negative 'what I'm afraid of' and 'what I can't stand' focuses are:

past	present	future
_____	_____	_____
_____	_____	_____
_____	_____	_____
_____	_____	_____

Add to these if you think of any more as we continue. I doubt that you had to think for long or dig very deep to find them. We often unearth quite a few once we start to become aware of them. Now, let's get constructive and positively focused. Use this part of the exercise to build a solid foundation for future focusing, that is, what you do well and what you have done well. Remember that the everyday little things are just as important as the larger things that you do well and see as your particular skills and strengths. Do not leave out things just because you expect them of yourself. Include everything you can on the list, such as the fact that you may be neat and tidy, generally thoughtful of others, etc.

My positive 'I can do/ I have done well/ I can cope' focuses are:

past	present	future
_____	_____	_____
_____	_____	_____
_____	_____	_____
_____	_____	_____

You will probably be surprised at how many you had forgotten about. If you haven't come up with a pretty impressive list, you also need to read another of my books in the *Sorting Out* series, *Sorting out Self-Esteem*. Don't despair—grab someone who knows you well right now, or in the very near future, and get that person to give you a hand to complete the list. Keep the list as specific as possible.

Now for the crunch. You need to make a determined pact with yourself that from this very moment in time onwards, you are going to focus on those things that you have done and can do, that will stand you in good stead to deal with any changes that are occurring or may occur in your life. You need to build on those things, so that you guide yourself towards the things in life that you wish to accomplish and achieve. If you lose the focus, and of course you will from time to time, it's no big deal; draw your focus and attention back to those things you can do, and have done well and run them through your 'self-talk' in your mind; store them in your memory bank for when you will need them in the future. Copy the list you have just made and carry it with you in your wallet or purse. A quick checklist can often save a lot of worry and unnecessary anxiety because we can easily get to it and quickly read through it to help us re-focus.

This is an easy-to-use technique which will help you take common sense into common practice. Common sense usually tells us that we can and will cope with the changes we encounter in life. You will find that your emotional state changes as you go through the focusing exercise. Optimism and a sense of 'yes, I can survive this and make the most of it' will begin to take over from what may have been an overriding sense of doom, anxiety and gloom. All the knowledge, education and ability in the world is worth absolutely nothing to us unless we use it in a very practical and regular manner for ourselves. Focusing is very strongly linked to self-esteem. When we focus positively we feel positive; when we focus poorly, we feel poorly. The choice is yours. Choose wisely!

QUICK RELAXATION TECHNIQUE

Now that we have begun the journey of keeping things positively focused, we need to take a little time to ensure that we remain as relaxed as we possibly can. This helps with our ability to focus on the positive and to use effective problem-solving and decision-making skills. Psychologically, relaxation is extremely important in assisting us to cope with all sorts of change in our lives. The research has been carried out over a long period of time and shows many benefits, not the least of which is our increased ability to think clearer and make better decisions. Other benefits include a change in brain waves, a healthier amount of adrenalin released into the body and a more efficient immune system.

I am convinced that relaxation can cement in place our focus on keeping things in perspective, so we can take these positive and solution-orientated attitudes into positive actions and goal setting for ourselves. The quick relaxation technique I am about to introduce can be done regularly throughout the day. It is designed to last from two to 10 minutes, and is best done in a comfortable chair with your eyes closed. However, parts of the technique can be used when preparing for any particular change, or driving towards an appointment you are late for.

The technique goes like this:

♦ Get yourself comfortable, loosen any tight clothing, remove glasses.

♦ When you are comfortable, let your muscles relax and unwind and then just concentrate on your body breathing.

♦ When you are ready, take a gentle deep breath and then sigh the breath out, as if you are sighing any worry, tension or concern out of your body. As you sigh the breath out say the word 'relax' to

yourself, smile and let all the muscles from your forehead to your feet go into floppy doll mode and unwind, relax and smooth out.

♦ Do the deep breathing routine three times.

♦ Then go back to breathing normally but continue with the word 'relax' as you breathe out, and continue to let those muscles relax and smooth out.

♦ Continue this for a few minutes and then use what is known as 'guided imagery' or visualisation to help you really unwind. Imagine yourself in a very pleasant place, like a beach, garden, holiday scene. Lie back feeling very relaxed, very much in control. This is your time to take care of yourself. If you find the imagery difficult, just feel how relaxed and calming it would be. Do this for several more minutes.

♦ Just before you open your eyes and gently move into the rest of the day, run two or three short positive self-talks through your head. Things like 'I am a worthwhile person' and 'I can cope well'.

♦ Slowly open your eyes, adjust to the light and gently move into the next activity in your day.

♦ If at all during the session you feel a little funny with your eyes closed, open your eyes for a short time, and then continue the technique when you are ready.

Longer relaxation techniques are also very good for us and can be very calming and useful. However, the compliance rate of people sticking to the longer techniques (generally 20 minutes) is very low. That's why I favour a shorter technique more often. Some of the useful longer techniques are things like deep muscle relaxation, autogenic training, transcendental meditation, self-hypnosis, yoga and tai chi. If you wish to pursue these, joining a group to do them may help you stick to them, so you gain the benefits over a longer period of time.

The two techniques just discussed, focusing and quick relaxation, can assist in both recovering from change and refocusing. Later on, we will look at the techniques of *thought stopping* and *thought switching*, which are extremely important in developing attitudinal efficiency. They will in turn play an essential role in your ability to recover, refocus and regenerate from any change in your life. But first, let's have a look at the meaning and relevance of *attitudinal efficiency*.

ATTITUDINAL EFFICIENCY

Deciding to get on top of change is a very positive step. Unfortunately, some people never manage to come to terms with it. One of the reasons that change in our lives can cause such chaos is that we are very quick to chastise ourselves and to focus on what we have done wrong, or why we will not be able to cope. Too often however, we overlook the reasons why we can and will be able to cope quite well. So we need to be aware of our achievements in life and remind ourselves that this will stand us in good stead to go on and achieve again even if the present seems a little uncertain. We need to lay a very firm and healthy foundation for our self-esteem, self-dignity and self-confidence levels. These aspects of our being are crucial if we are to have a high quality of life and deal with change effectively.

ATTITUDES, BELIEFS AND COPING WITH CHANGE

There is no doubt that the most critical component of dealing effectively with any change in life is the mind. The amazing fact is that we tend to spend so little time training and coaching it correctly. We tend to fill it up with inflexible, irrational, negative and upsetting attitudes and beliefs about things, especially about certain changes that may occur in our lives. We can then have a lot of trouble recalling any positive and rational thoughts and feelings when we most need them.

So how do we train and coach our mind to be our best friend when dealing with the distress of particular changes in life? The answer is simple, the same way we would train a sportsperson, a musician, a dancer—by practising the proper skills necessary to cope effectively with things such as change. It's the same with our thinking, attitudes and beliefs. We need to practise the skills that will help us deal with these three aspects of our being as well as possible. To ensure that we develop *attitudinal efficiency* we must make sure that our attitudes and beliefs are flexible, adaptable, rational, positive and solution-orientated. As the philosopher Epictetus (AD 50-138) inscribed on a stone tablet: *'Life is not about happenings, but what people tell themselves about those happenings'*.

Epictetus hit the nail right on the head. Having the right sorts of attitudes and beliefs about the situations which happen in our lives is certainly important if we are to feel a sense of control over ourselves and our reactions to whatever changes are happening.

The reality is that the same event happening to two different people can receive a totally different reaction from each person. One may be very calm and quite relaxed, while the other person may have an anxiety attack over it. Why does the same situation elicit different responses from different people? It primarily has to do with the 'tape recorder' up there in your head. I will explain about the tape recorder and its role in coping with changes a little further on. Before I do that, I need to go back a step or two.

Around any changing situation or event that can happen in our lives there are three time periods which are important:

♦ before the event or change actually happens;

♦ during the event or change; and

♦ after the change.

Before the change some of us may begin to conjure up real nightmares.

CASE STUDY

Barry, 25, had been working in his position for 18 months when his manager called him into the office. His manager informed him that the whole department was being restructured and that unfortunately Barry was being made redundant. Barry had far too much alcohol that night and woke up the next morning in a panic. He thought that any chance of a career was gone and also wondered what people would think about him being made redundant. He started to think that his friends might think he'd lost his job because he was incompetent.

Barry eventually told his best mate that he had been made redundant and found out that his friend's girlfriend had just been retrenched also. Barry immediately felt 'normal' again, and not like some loser. Three weeks after leaving his old job Barry scored a new position which involved travelling overseas two or three times a year and paid $6000 more than his last one. Barry realised change was not so bad after all.

Of course there is no rational reason to make a 'nightmare' out of an event such as retrenchment, but if we do not monitor ourselves we certainly can. When we tell ourselves negative, irrational and stressful things about an event—'it will be terrible, I can't stand it'—then our behaviour will become affected. We may begin to shake, perspire and perhaps stutter a little. This can then heighten our worry and concerns and increase our stress levels even further. Emotionally we can become quite upset, worried and distressed.

If you allow yourself to get like that before any change, what hope do you have of remaining calm and relaxed during the change process? Very little, unless you know how to get your reactions back under your control and calm yourself down effectively. This of course is quite possible. Naturally, it is better if we do not allow ourselves to panic and lose the plot in the first place. How we react to any particular change in our life is very important, as it can play a major part in how we react to the next change, especially a similar one. If, following a particular change, we feel anxious, worried or upset, then we are likely to feel that way again when a similar change is about to happen.

From any change occurring in our lives—before, during or after the change—there will be consequences which will impact on our behaviour (actions), our thinking (attitudes and beliefs) and our emotions (feelings or moods). If a positive change happens, we will tend to act, think and feel happy. If a negative change occurs, we tend to act, think and feel sad or depressed.

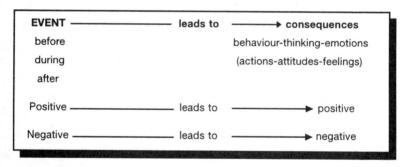

Now take a few moments to consider your own profile. The idea is to work fairly quickly through the following process:

What changes have there been in your life that you have felt very stressed about before they happened? Or are there any changes that may happen and that you are very concerned about now?

_____

_____

_____

Have you been aware of the symptoms and consequences of this worry and concern for you? If so, what are they?

_____

_____

_____

_____

Have there been changes that left you really 'strung out' afterwards?

_____

_____

_____

As you know, different people do have totally different reactions to exactly the same change or changes happening in their lives. Why is this? Well, how we react to any change in our lives depends upon what we have stored on that tape recorder in our heads that I mentioned earlier—the memory banks in our brain.

I want you to imagine that up there in your head you do indeed have a tape recorder with a tape in it. That tape contains your *memory banks*—all those life experiences from your past and present and your expectations of the future are stored on that tape in your long-term memory storage. From all this

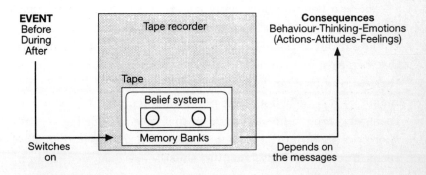

EVENT
Before
During
After

Switches
on

Tape recorder

Tape

Belief system

○   ○

Memory Banks

Consequences
Behaviour-Thinking-Emotions
(Actions-Attitudes-Feelings)

Depends on
the messages

information you have developed attitudes, beliefs, values, judgments and perceptions about what life is all about and how it 'should' or 'must' be. The information stored on your tape is sometimes referred to as forming a 'belief system'.

What occurs is that a change is about to happen, is happening or has just happened. The tape recorder in your head then switches on and plays you messages about the change. Now, what comes out of the tape will depend on what is stored there, and this will in turn affect your ongoing behaviour, thoughts and emotions. If positive attitudes and beliefs are released, then the consequences will be positive. If, on the other hand, negative and irrational beliefs and judgments are made, the consequences, in terms of your behaviour, thoughts and emotions are likely to be quite negative, such as worry, anxiety and ongoing uncertainty.

WHERE DID ALL THOSE ATTITUDES AND BELIEFS STORED IN OUR BELIEF SYSTEMS COME FROM?

It usually starts with the values and beliefs our parents brought us up with. It continues with the influence of our peers, what our mates were into at school, school teachers, work mates, sporting or artistic heroes. Literally all our experiences throughout life are included in the formation of our belief systems. We then form these into ways of making judgments about the world, how it ought to or should be in our view, including what should or must happen for us to feel at ease or okay.

You can imagine how many beliefs involving uncertainties and fears are stored in those tapes—beliefs that if not controlled, changed and replaced, could cause ongoing high levels of distress, even in situations that are not major catastrophes, life-threatening or even dangerous in any way. There are many major irrational beliefs that human beings tend to collect on their way through life and store on that tape in their heads, and there are also many common distorted thinking styles. The techniques we will be learning shortly are designed to gain awareness and control over any of these beliefs that may pop out during periods of change in our life.

Let's have a look at some of those irrational and distorted beliefs, particularly as they relate to change in our lives. No one, hopefully, has all of these at the same time and the ones we do have, we have them in varying degrees from a little to a lot. However, as mentioned earlier, these sorts of distorted thinking styles are stored up in that tape recorder in our heads ready to pop out and cause us all sorts of upset if we allow them to.

SELF-TALK (ATTITUDES AND BELIEFS)— COMMON IRRATIONAL BELIEFS REGARDING CHANGE

Dr Albert Ellis, an American psychologist who is well known as the father of rational emotive therapy, has formulated a number of the most common irrational beliefs that people hold. Some of these apply to people trying to cope with change of one type or another in their life. They are:

- ◆ I must be loved, or at least liked and approved of by every significant person I meet.

- ◆ I must be completely competent, make no mistakes and achieve in every possible way if I am to be okay.

- ◆ It is dreadful, nearly the end of the world when things are not as I would like them to be.

- ◆ Human unhappiness, including mine, is caused by factors outside of my control, so little can be done about it.

- ◆ If something might be unpleasant or frightening I should worry about it a great deal.

- ◆ It's easier to put off doing something unpleasant than it is to face up to it.

- ◆ I need someone stronger than myself to depend on.

As I stated earlier, it is unlikely that you would have all these irrational beliefs, and the ones you may have would also vary in the degree to which you hold them in your belief system.

Now let's consider some *distorted thinking styles* and how they affect our ability to cope effectively with change.

DISTORTED THINKING STYLES

♦ *Filtering*—looking at the change through dark-coloured glasses. This is where you take and magnify the negatives in a situation and forget about the positives.

♦ *Catastrophising*—this is a style of thinking where we 'expect the worst'. You expect to not cope well and then talk yourself into not coping well. It is sometimes called the 'what if, syndrome'— 'what if I can't cope?', 'what if I am never happy again?', 'what if I don't get another job?', 'what if I don't find another partner?'.

Another form of catastrophising is 'making mountains out of molehills'. This occurs when we exaggerate what is happening and treat an everyday event as if it is a dreadful and terrible happening.

♦ *Blaming*—we hold other people responsible for the pain or unhappiness we are feeling—'it's your fault, you make me feel upset or angry'. Of course the blaming may also go inwards, 'I'm hopeless and useless, I have no value as a person'.

♦ *Shoulds and Musts*—some people use 'shoulds and musts' as if there is some universal law to back them up. 'You should do the right thing by me', 'I must alway be in control and have things the way I want them'. Where is this universal law written? Of course there is no universal law!

What irrational beliefs and distorted thinking styles are you aware of that you carry around in your belief system, especially with regard to coping with changes in your life?

_____

_____

_____

_____

There are obviously more distorted thinking styles, but these will serve our purpose for now. If we have even a few of these types of beliefs floating around on that tape in our heads (the place we store our interpretations of our life experiences in the form of beliefs about how things ought to be), they can cause us to deal extremely poorly with change and to be affected by it very negatively.

In chapters 3 and 4 I talked about the stages of change people often go through when a change is occurring in their lives (Chapter 3) and the stages of readiness to deal with or accept the change (Chapter 4). Later in this chapter I will get you to consider these, and the irrational and distorted attitudes and beliefs that may be associated with certain stages, as well as the more rational and positive attitudes and beliefs that may be associated with other particular stages.

Right now we will look at a technique to deal with those irrational beliefs.

THOUGHT STOPPING AND THOUGHT SWITCHING

This is a method of gaining control over your attitudes and your belief system in order to buffer yourself against the emotional turmoil often associated with coping with change. You will need a reasonably large rubber band, which is big enough to fit very comfortably on your wrist. Once you have placed the rubber band on one of your wrists we are ready to begin.

Step 1—Think of a particular change that is occurring in your life or may occur and then become aware of what you are telling yourself. If you find yourself feeling a little anxious and thinking things like 'it would be terrible', 'how on earth would I cope', then:

Step 2—Flick yourself gently with the rubber band. This is purely to make sure you have got your own attention. It is not to punish yourself for using catastrophising and negative self-talk and beliefs.

Step 3—Now imagine a small 'stop' sign coming up in front of your face and firmly say the word 'stop' to yourself . You are stopping that tape recorder in your head running on with all those negative and self-defeating thoughts and beliefs.

Step 4—Imagine the click of a switch in your head. This means you are switching your thinking from the negative, upsetting thoughts to more flexible, adaptable, rational, positive and solution orientated thinking. You can remember how to think this way by using the acronym (first letter of each word) FARPS:

Flexible;

Adaptable;

Rational;

Positive;

Solution-oriented

Start **FARPS**ing regularly, it's good for you.

Step 5—You have stopped the tape. Now say four or five short 'self-talks'—things like 'I would rather this was not happening, but I need to accept that it is', 'what is the best thing I can do to make it work for me?', 'I can cope with this', 'you watch me make it work out for the best'.

What you have now done is to tape messages that are going to work for you, and assist you in dealing with whatever is happening. You then have those messages and beliefs on your tape for next time, so when something happens in the future, the messages that pop out of your tape will be far more positive, rational and solution-orientated. It really is not that difficult; all it takes is:

◆ the desire to do it;

◆ remembering to do it early on (you now have the rubber band on your wrist to remind you);

◆ practise, practise, practise—just like the professional sportsperson.

A little more clarification about each of the areas of FARPS follows:

◆ *flexible*—you see the big picture, other people's points of view, getting as many facts as possible, and you have the willingness to learn;

◆ *adaptable*—you have an ability and willingness to change if need be, rather than being defensive and blocking off new ideas;

◆ *rational*—you keep things in perspective. There are no 'shoulds' or 'musts';

◆ *positive*—'I can . . . I am able to . . . how do I? . . . I will get on top of this';

◆ *solution-oriented*—'what is the best thing to do right now?'. You look for the best things to do to get a positive resolution, without becoming oppositional, blaming or indulging in the 'poor me' syndrome.

FARPSing is something we need to practise on a very regular basis if we are to become very effective at coping with whatever life throws our way. For some people FARPSing is something they will already be very good at, but for most of us there is certainly work to be done in that area. Now, what happens to those irrational beliefs and distorted thinking styles when you use FARPS and the thought stopping and thought switching technique? Well, let's see:

FAR MORE RATIONAL BELIEFS

Compare these to the irrational beliefs noted earlier on page 64:

♦ I need to be loved and liked by some of the important people in my life. When some don't, I may feel disappointed but I can cope with that. I will do the best I can to develop and keep close friends and good relationships.

♦ I am a fallible human being and I cannot expect myself to always make the right decisions or handle everything perfectly. I won't make excuses; if I don't do well, I will look at why and try to do better next time and as I go.

♦ I will give life my best shot, including coping with change. If it doesn't always work out how I would like it to, well that's life. Getting all upset and stressed out won't help. What do I need to do to have things work out the best for me?

♦ Of course my problem may be influenced by things outside of my control, however my reactions are influenced by me! Now, what can I do about whatever it is that's changing?

♦ What good is worrying about the change going to do? I will take steps to prevent nasty things happening and then get on with life. The rest is up to fate and I can live with that.

♦ While I'm putting off dealing with it, it may be growing in size. There will be some anxiety in facing the change head on; however, if I plan a solution as well as I can and then do it, that is all I can do and I am going to give myself a pat on the back for getting into it.

♦ The person I need to rely most on is me. At times I will need support from others, and I feel okay about that. If I don't get it, I will seek it elsewhere.

Thinking and developing beliefs and attitudes like these means that change can be dealt with very constructively and in a timely manner without all the negative self-talk and related stress on us. When we practise these the rewards are wonderful, with the result that we feel far more in control of our life generally.

Now, what can we do to correct those Distorted Thinking Styles we noted on page 64?:

◆ *Filtering*—look at what you can do and have done in life, and use this to help you realise that you can cope well with any change in your life. List down the things you do well—even the little things. Learn from what you can't do and haven't done and see it as a challenge. Catch yourself being good.

◆ *Catastrophising*—so what if something does happen? Will you be able to stop it? If the answer is *yes*, stop it now; if not, be aware of what you might need to cope with and return to your normal day's activity. The catastrophe scale, which I will go over as the next coping technique will also help keep things in perspective.

◆ *Blaming*—don't fall into any form of victim trap by blaming others or yourself. Let it go, it is all part of the journey of life. Take on the ownership of resolving the problem—'if it's to be, it's up to me'.

◆ *Shoulds and Musts*—as I have stated earlier, there is no universal law saying we or others 'should' or 'must'. Shoulds and musts stress us out, and may lead us into blaming ourselves or others for what is happening, and trying to make others feel guilty about something . It is far better to use statements like 'I would like you to' or 'I will give it my best shot'. These are rational and positive statements without the 'you should' or 'I must' involved.

If you remain aware and practise techniques like the thought stopping and thought switching techniques, you can also learn to rid yourself of the distorted thinking styles which are a major cause of stress within us.

THE EQUATION:
SUCCESS = PRACTICE X PERSISTENCE

I have talked about the necessity for practice when beginning to use these positive and adaptive attitudinal techniques. Here is one way to get started and make sure you are on the right track. This exercise will assist you by focusing you on:

◆ what is happening;

◆ what you can do about it; and

◆ the benefits for you at the end of it all.

The following technique was originally the work of Dr Albert Ellis who I mentioned earlier on. You can use the actual exercise that follows to work through a 'real life' situation involving a change you have experienced that you felt very stressed about. You may photocopy it or enlarge it, and use the procedure in future situations to help keep you on track with your attitudes and beliefs.

You really need plenty of flexible, adaptable, rational, positive and solution-oriented attitudes and beliefs stored on that tape recorder up there in your head.

The procedure to practise is:

1. *Identify the situation of concern*, for example, you have just lost your job.

2. *What are your irrational and upsetting self-talks (beliefs)?* for example 'it's the end of the world, I am hopeless, I will never get another decent job, no one would want to employ me, my life is ruined'.

3. *Actions resulting from those thoughts:*	*Emotions resulting from those thoughts:*
Drink too much alcohol	Intense sadness, panic and
Withdraw, tearful, moody	anxiety
Don't look for another job	Feelings of worthlessness, low self-esteem

4. *Dispute the upsetting beliefs*, that is, use FARPS. Realise that while something may be an unfortunate event, it is not the end of the world. Take the opportunity to take stock of what you would like to do with your life. Look at the options and you may discover some wonderful opportunities. Use attitudes like 'I have skills and I am willing to work' and 'there are greater challenges I could face in life'.

5. *List the effects of FARPSing*, that is, the benefits of disputing the irrational/upsetting beliefs:

Actions / Behaviours:	Beliefs / Attitudes:	Emotions / Feelings:
Relaxed, less tense	I will find another job	Appropriate sadness and anxiety
Get your resume up to date	It is an opportunity	Calm, enjoy the challenge
Keep things in perspective	I am okay	Apprehension and excitement

This is just an example of how you need to work through the following exercise.

Now it's your turn. Choose your own situation to work through.

1. Identify the situation of concern:

_____

_____

_____

2. Irrational and upsetting beliefs:

_____

_____

_____

_____

3. Actions resulting from these types of beliefs:

_____

_____

_____

_____

Emotions resulting from these types of beliefs:

_____

_____

_____

_____

4. Dispute the upsetting beliefs, that is, use more flexible, adaptable, rational, positive, and solution-oriented thinking:

_____

_____

_____

5. List the effects of disputing the irrational/upsetting beliefs:

Actions/Behaviours	Beliefs/Attitudes	Emotions/Feelings
_____	_____	_____
_____	_____	_____
_____	_____	_____

Remember that practice makes the common *sense* of rational and positive beliefs translate into common *practice*. By using the above technique you will gain:

♦ personal control;

♦ fewer symptoms of distress;

♦ positive focus;

♦ higher self-esteem;

♦ fulfilment;

♦ happiness;

♦ contentedness;

♦ control of your own destiny.

And of course all these benefits condense into one major personal gain—higher quality of life.

While the thought stopping and thought switching technique may appear to be common sense, you cannot assume that you will automatically think or perceive situations involving change this rationally. This technique helps take common sense into common practice, so make sure you are very adept at remaining positive and solution-orientated. Make sure that you control that tape recorder up there in your head. The benefits are not only there for yourself, but for all those around you. Others will see a person who is:

- more relaxed;
- more fun;
- more rational;
- more optimistic;
- more self-assured.

We often tell ourselves not to think so negatively and how stupid we are for thinking like that. However we seldom then start thinking in the positive manner I have just been through. This is the critical component of what I have just been talking about and what I refer to as *attitudinal efficiency*. It is no good just to stop the negatives and the ridiculing of ourselves—that is only the start. It is the implementing of the positives and solutions that makes the difference to our coping capabilities.

THE CATASTROPHE SCALE

KEEPING THINGS IN PERSPECTIVE

This technique is called the *catastrophe scale*. It is both straightforward and easy to remember, and is aimed at helping you keep things in perspective. Using imagery or visualisation is the key to using the scale. It's the same as imagining the tape recorder—imagine it as a small ruler sitting up there in the front of your head. The ruler is marked or calibrated from 0-100.

Now, in terms of a real catastrophe in life, 10 on the scale is something minor, 25 would be a pain, 50 is something more serious, 75 is getting reasonably more serious and 90 is something that is pretty nasty that could happen to you, such as the death of someone very close to us, being made a quadriplegic or paraplegic in an accident, or the diagnosis of a terminal illness. Those things would rate in the 90s on the scale. In reality then, retrenchment from a job or your partner leaving you would rate 50 to 75 compared with the diagnosis of a terminal illness or being severely injured in an accident. Dropping a plate in the kitchen would of course, in comparison rate a 2. The picture by now ought to be coming clearer.

Most things that happen to us on a day to day basis probably rate somewhere between 2 and 20. However, if we do not keep things in perspective, our reactions to these everyday happenings could be up around the 90 mark.

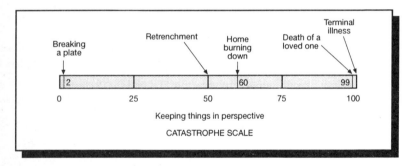

The idea then, is to quickly remind ourselves of the reality of what is happening. If what is happening is around 10 out of 100 in terms of what could happen to us, we need to bring our reaction back to a rating of 10 also.

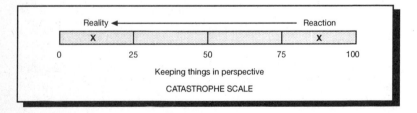

Calm it down, keep things in perspective and forget about the exaggerations.

To assist in stopping the catastrophising thoughts, you can use the thought stopping and thought switching technique. Flick yourself gently with the rubber band, imagine that stop sign coming up in front of your face and firmly say the word 'stop'. Then switch your thinking to assist you in keeping things in perspective. Run four or five short self-talks through that tape recorder in your head concerning the reality of this change in your life and make sure you calm yourself down and then look for the best solution.

As an aid in recognising those things you tend to let get out of perspective, let's spend a few minutes considering what they are:

Things I regularly blow out of perspective:

_____

_____

_____

Regarding recent changes in my life, things I blow out of perspective are/were:

_____

_____

_____

_____

Sometimes a little thought is required to find them but they certainly are there and need flushing out and then dealing with. It can be a useful self-discovery process to spend a few minutes digging them out. Once you have discovered what these fairly common 'loss of perspective' situations are, it is far easier to remember, be aware of, and pull yourself up if you are tending to slip into them.

From the list of things that you tend to get out of perspective, what are two that you are going to focus on and use the catastrophe scale to help keep them far more in perspective for yourself?

I need to keep an eye on and de-catastrophise:

_____

_____

_____

SUMMARY

◆ We need to develop emotional, attitudinal and behavioural control.

◆ Following major life changes you need to apply the 3R rule:

- recover;

- refocus; and

- regenerate.

◆ Emotional maturity means that our feelings are governed by rational thinking and behaviour. It is the ability to remain calm, positively focused and solution-oriented no matter what happens in life.

◆ Emotional maturity test—how did you fare?

◆ Use *focusing* to gain emotional control.

◆ Quick relaxation technique—use it regularly.

◆ Attitudinal efficiency—remember the tape recorder in your head.

◆ You need to keep your beliefs:

- Flexible;

- Adaptable;

- Rational;

- Positive;

- Solution-oriented.

- Self-talk—there are seven common irrational beliefs regarding change.

- Distorted thinking styles—four examples are:
  - filtering;
  - catastrophising;
  - blaming;
  - 'shoulds' and 'musts'.

- Remember the thought stopping and thought switching technique using the rubber band.

- Develop more rational beliefs by disputing irrational beliefs.

- Equation: Success = practice × persistence.

- Disputing irrational beliefs leads to a greater sense of:
  - personal control;
  - fewer symptoms of distress;
  - positive focus;
  - higher self-esteem;
  - fulfilment;
  - happiness;
  - contentedness;
  - control of destiny.

- The catastrophe scale helps to keep things in perspective.

CHAPTER 7

Practical problem-solving and dealing with change

In the last chapter we learnt about some techniques which can assist us greatly in keeping our emotions and our attitudes rational and positive during periods of change, or for that matter, at any time in our lives. Our behaviour will also be affected by these techniques, because if our emotions and attitudes are more in control our behaviour will tend to automatically follow. Later in this chapter we will consider a very practical problem-solving model which will allow us to keep our behaviour and actions positive and solution-oriented during any period of change in any area of our lives.

First, we are going to use the coping techniques we have just been exposed to in the last chapter, to help us deal with the specific stages of change we can spiral through and the stages of readiness for change. If we don't learn to use effective ways of dealing with the particular issues in these stages we will probably get caught in a particular stage, or see-saw between several.

In Chapter 3, I gave you a picture of the four stages of change, these were:

◆ stage 1—loss phase;

◆ stage 2—emotional phase;

◆ stage 3—exploration phase; and

◆ stage 4—acceptance and commitment.

If neglected, the first two stages can have quite a devastating effect, so let's consider them carefully and the attitudes and beliefs we need to develop and maintain to deal effectively with whatever is happening.

STAGE 1—LOSS PHASE

Often characterised by shock and denial, this phase lasts for varying periods of time depending on the individual. It is also generally characterised by a dulling of emotions and the senses. Some people describe it as feeling depersonalised—they feel as if they are not really with themselves. Shock is a very real phenomenon for people who experience unexpected change in life, such as the sudden death of a loved one or a retrenchment out of the blue. So, how do you deal as effectively as possible with this stage of change? Here are the five golden rules:

1. Accept that you will feel different for a while and that it is your turn to look after yourself.

2. Use friends and loved ones for support and comfort during this phase.

3. Keep up as much of your normal lifestyle going as is possible,

but expect to be less effective or in touch with things as you normally are.

4. Don't overindulge in alcohol or any prescribed or non-prescribed drugs as you come to grips with what has happened.

5. Gently work on keeping your attitudes as positive and rational as possible.

To practise the last point try the following exercise:

Typical 'normal' upsetting thoughts during this phase would be:

_____

_____

Irrational and catastrophising thoughts during this time might be:

_____

_____

_____

More rational and solution-orientated beliefs to work on during this time would be:

_____

_____

_____

_____

STAGE 2—EMOTIONAL PHASE

This stage is characterised by heightened emotional responses and a very real resistance to accepting the change or changes. The common emotions during this time are anger, anxiety, fear and depression. Thoughts can include:

◆ 'how dare they';

◆ 'I can't cope with this';

- 'I will make them pay';
- 'they shouldn't have done this';
- 'my life is over';
- 'I will never find anyone else like him/her'.

Here are five golden rules for dealing constructively with this stage:

- Accept the fact that what has happened has happened and life is like that—things will not always go as you would like them to.
- Take the *ownership* for getting your life back on track.
- Accept how you feel, but acknowledge that you are going to control this and not fall into a victim trap.
- Use the FARPS thought stopping and switching technique to keep your attitudes under control.
- Use the problem-solving technique described later in this chapter to move onto the next stage—exploration.

Here is a quick exercise to help you with the fourth golden rule. Consider the following:

Irrational, rigid and upsetting beliefs and thoughts during this phase:

_____

_____

_____

_____

Far more rational, positive and solution-orientated beliefs and thoughts:

_____

_____

_____

_____

STAGES OF READINESS

Let's now move to the stages of readiness for change discussed in Chapter 4.

There are five stages that people seem to go through on a regular basis:

- pre-contemplation;
- contemplation;
- preparation;
- action;
- maintenance.

We will deal with the first three here. Now it does not take a genius to realise that if you get stuck in any of the first three stages, especially the first two, you will have, or continue to have, trouble coping and adapting effectively to change. So what are the golden rules for ensuring you do not get stuck? Let's look at the first stage of readiness.

PRE-CONTEMPLATION

1 This is the stage where we are in a comfort zone and usually happy with what is happening. Then all of a sudden—change! Whether it is personal or work-related does not really matter. Now, we could be in this stage because the change comes out of the blue, or perhaps because we have avoided signs that something was going to happen—we may not have wanted to consider the possibility. The five golden rules for moving on from this stage are:

1. Face the fact that events that we may not want to happen, can occur at any time in our lives. Be prepared.

2. Look at why you may be resisting change. What are you really worried about or fearful of?

3. Remain adaptable not defensive during your life. Be open to the advantages that particular changes may offer you.

4. Enjoy working with and learning from others to better yourself.

5. Use FARPS to help you dispute attitudes which may be hampering your acceptance of the change.

The following exercise will assist you to institute the fifth golden rule. Consider the following:

Reasons I am resistant to change:

_____

_____

_____

Disputing—advantages that will, or may, come out of the change:

_____

_____

_____

CONTEMPLATION

2 This is the stage where we begin to feel that the change may offer certain opportunities and may not be quite as nasty as we originally thought. We may see or hear of others who have benefited from similar circumstances in their lives.

This stage is full of see-sawing thinking 'yes I will, no I won't' or 'I think I can, I'm not sure I can'. Here are five more golden rules to help you cope with this stage and move on to *preparation:*

1. We do not always achieve what we want the first time; 'stickability' is often needed.

2. Focus on the advantages of changing and the disadvantages of not changing, rather than on the advantages of not changing and the disadvantages of changing.

3. Make a list of the strengths you have—the things you do well and have done well in your life. Refer to these regularly.

4. Do not allow yourself to fall into the 'victim trap'—take ownership for changing.

5. Use FARPS to keep your attitudes and beliefs positive, rational and solution-oriented.

   Use this exercise to help you crispen your fifth golden rule here:

What realistic anxieties and fears might you feel in this stage?

_____

_____

_____

_____

What unrealistic concerns might you develop?

_____

_____

_____

_____

Dispute—change the unrealistic concerns to positive and adaptive attitudes and beliefs:

_____

_____

_____

PREPARATION

3 The preparation stage is where a commitment to making the best of the change has been made and the 'how to' is now the issue. The five golden rules at this stage are:

1. Focus on what you need to do to make a success of things.

2. Gain information from others on how they have coped and what they have done.

3. Implement solutions gradually and with persistence.

4. Aim to 'unfreeze' old habits and 'refreeze' new habits in their place.

5. Formulate a problem-solving action plan and use it to guide you through the change.

Use the readiness for change quiz in Chapter 4 as a guide to which stage you are most likely to be in, and hence which of the golden rules you may most have to focus on. It is like anything else in life, the more in control of something we feel we are, the better we cope and deal with it.

This is a phenomenon that psychologists have called *self-efficacy*. Basically, the more self-efficacy you feel, the greater the likelihood that you will be able to do something and do it well. Self-efficacy towards any particular event about to happen in life is generally related to how well you have handled similar events in the past.

This is where practice in handling change is important. We need to desensitise ourselves to the fear of change—rather than avoiding it because it provokes such anxiety within us.

SOLVING PROBLEMS AND MAKING DECISIONS

If we are to be effective managers of change in our life, we are going to need good problem-solving and decision-making skills.

Let's now work through the steps involved in making effective decisions for ourselves. Keep in mind that for some of you this process may seem a little tedious. Once you have done it a few times you can then become a little less formal about the process. You will then tend to do it more on automatic pilot.

If we don't take the time to learn how to do things properly, we often rush through them, leave out important processes, make poor decisions and then worry about the poor results we obtained. We may serve to reinforce that we cannot cope. Remember the old saying 'an ounce of prevention is worth a pound of cure'.

So let's slow ourselves down and use the opportunity to fine-tune our decision-making and problem-solving skills.

Step 1—What is the change/challenge I want to cope with effectively? Be specific, for example, 'rebuild a new life after divorce' or 'handle the retrenchment well'. 'My goal is...':

_____

_____

_____

Step 2—How do I feel about it all? For example, uncertain, excited, confused, anxious, energised, etc:

_____

_____

_____

Step 3—Relax, unwind for a moment. Make sure you are not frowning, tense or frustrated. If so, use the quick relaxation technique to unwind.

Decision-making and problem-solving need to be fun and exhilarating, a normal part of life. Learn to enjoy the challenge of embarking on new adventures and to relax while doing them.

Step 4—Consider all possible solutions. Can you think of different ways of achieving a positive outcome? List down the different things you could do, and different ways you could go about it.

_____

_____

_____

_____

Step 5—How might others go about achieving this goal?

_____

_____

_____

_____

Step 6—List the things you could do in order of priority with, 1 being your best idea, 2 your second best etc.

_____

_____

_____

_____

Step 7—Make a choice. Select which option you will take. It may not be number 1 on your list, it may be another option. I am going to:

_____

_____

Step 8—How will you do it? Form a plan of action. I need to:

- _____
- _____
- _____
- _____
- _____
- _____
- _____

Step 9—When are you going to start this process? Set a date.

I will begin on: _____

I will review my progress on: _____

Step 10—Give yourself a pat on the back

Well done. You certainly deserve that pat on the back and you need to make sure you give it to yourself because others may forget to. Now an interesting point. Can you think of any benefits to you of having the particular challenge in your life?

One I can think of is that it has led you to get to this stage of understanding; there is no need to worry or procrastinate about things—just settle down and work out a solution as you have just done.

Here's a tip—remember to use what ever support networks there are available to you, including professional services if you need them.

SUMMARY

◆ We can learn to cope effectively by developing positive attitudes and beliefs as we move through the four phases of the change spiral.

◆ Remember the five golden rules for coping in the first two phases of the spiral.

◆ We looked at three stages of readiness for change:

- pre-contemplation;

- contemplation; and

- preparation.

Remember how to move through each one of them.

◆ Use the 10-step strategy for solving problems and making decisions.

CHAPTER 8

Helping others to cope

There are many situations in life when we do indeed get the opportunity to assist others in coping with changes in their lives. Not only is it a very rewarding and empathic thing to do for others, but the helper can also learn an awful lot about adapting to, and coping with change from assisting others to do their best.

So let's have a look at the different changes that can occur in people's life and how we may assist them in coping with these changes, in the different roles we may be fulfilling.

CHANGE 1—DEATH OF A LOVED ONE
In the role of a spouse or partner:

◆ be tolerant and understanding of the person's feelings;

◆ allow your partner time to grieve and recover gently;

◆ keep as normal a lifestyle as possible going for the person;

- do not make judgments about how the person should cope;
- encourage your partner to keep photos and other items of his or her loved one displayed and in plain view.

In the role of a friend:

- support and spend time with your friend;
- do not make value judgments about how your friend should cope;
- be empathic (understanding) but not sympathetic (overly emotional);
- remain a helper, not a rescuer—you could end up a victim yourself;
- offer advice if requested, otherwise just listen.

In the role of a manager / supervisor at work:

- show support and empathy for the person;
- allow reasonable time for the person to recover;
- ask the person what he or she would like the staff to know;
- follow up with the person to show concern;
- if necessary, utilise internal or external support services.

CHANGE 2—RETRENCHMENT FROM A JOB

In the role of a manager or supervisor:

- provide information on what is happening in a timely manner and mobilise support services available;
- follow up to show support;
- act as a referee for the person if appropriate;
- protect the confidentiality of the person.

In the role of a spouse or partner:

- be empathic and acknowledge fears and concerns;
- assist the person in remaining solution-oriented;

- keep as normal a lifestyle as possible going;
- assist in keeping things in perspective, and be careful about catastrophising;
- provide positive feedback to help keep self-esteem high.

In the role of a friend:

- insist your friend keep up his or her social activities;
- elicit the assistance of other friends in supporting the person;
- do not get into blaming others for what has happened;
- be positive and solution-oriented in your interaction;
- reinforce the positive qualities of the person.

CHANGE 3—RELATIONSHIP BREAKDOWN
In the role of the spouse or partner:

- remain as rational as possible and do not be overly emotional;
- do not character assassinate the person;
- rebuild your new life, and forget about 'continuing the crisis';
- where possible support the person in rebuilding his or her life;
- do not use friends or children to get at your ex-partner.

In the role of a friend:

- be empathic with the person rather than sympathetic;
- be careful about 'taking sides';
- help the person to see solutions and rebuild his or her lifestyle;
- do things together—do not let them wallow in a 'poor me' syndrome;
- take the role of an objective outsider—do not blame.

In the role of a manager or supervisor:

- stay within your counselling limitations;
- suggest support services available within the company;

◆ do not moralise or make too many value judgments;

◆ focus on work performance problems if there are any, not on the personal issues;

◆ allow some time for the emotional upheaval to settle.

ASSISTING INDIVIDUALS TO HANDLE CHANGE

When we are in any sort of support role with a person experiencing a fair amount of change in his or her life, we need to assist that person to:

◆ recover;

◆ refocus; and

◆ regenerate.

The recovering process is where the person regains a sense of balance and routine. Help them use time to do things they enjoy. A realistic perspective on life can be regained by focusing on the 'big picture'. What possibilities does this present? What has the person done and what can he or she do well? What opportunities and options are open to him or her?

The regenerating process involves assisting the person to get adequate rest, avoid excessive alcohol and eat properly. Help to increase the circle of support. Involve the person in social and re-creational pursuits. This is where assistance is needed in helping the person to rebuild a new lifestyle, to come to grips with what has happened, to accept that things will not be the way they were, and to rebuild their self-esteem and belief in the future.

ASSISTING GROUPS OF PEOPLE TO HANDLE CHANGE

When groups and teams of people are going through periods of change there may be a need for change in:

- information that is known and understood by people;
- procedures that people follow; or
- the inclination of people to perform in a particular way.

Remember that change involves leaving the known for the unknown, the familiar for the unfamiliar and the comfortable for the uncomfortable.

The management of change will depend on what phase of the change spiral people in the team or group are in (see Chapter 3).

LOSS PHASE

At this stage, just provide information on what is happening— all that is known at that time. Let them know that the change will happen. Explain what to expect and suggest actions they can take to adjust to the change. Give them time to let things sink in, then schedule a planning session to see how people are feeling and coping.

EMOTIONAL PHASE

At this stage, it is important that you listen, acknowledge feelings and uncertainties, respond empathically and encourage support among the team. Accept people's negative responses as legitimate and appropriate for this phase. Understand that as difficult as it seems, this phase will pass with time, so focus on recovery. Help people say good-bye to the old structures and ways by acknowledging their feelings of loss through the use of ritual. Say good-bye to the old ways and welcome the new ways.

EXPLORATION PHASE

Now, conduct brainstorming, visioning (our view for the future) and planning sessions. Discuss values and priorities, and help people see potential opportunities for the organisation and for themselves. Create a focus for creative energy by setting short-term goals.

ACCEPTANCE AND COMMITMENT PHASE

Now, it is time to set longer-term goals. An emphasis can now be placed on team building and team development activities. Make opportunities for creative problem-solving for the group, and assist them to develop those skills. Increase group involvement by using techniques aimed at enhancing empowerment (self-responsibility and decision-making). Validate and encourage those responding and adapting well to the change. Assist the team members to look ahead and enjoy the journey!

Here are some important considerations to bear in mind: *Individuality*—team members are obviously individuals and will respond in different ways at different times. There is no definite pattern of responding. This is why it is extremely important to manage the individual, as well as the team through times of change. Make sure you spend time with each member discussing his or her progress through the change process.

Hiccups and regressions—teams and individuals may be progressing well and suddenly an unexpected or unwelcome event will occur and they may return to an earlier phase in the change spiral. This classically occurs following something like a downsizing in a company, where things settle for a while and then everything is restructured. People begin to get worn out, demoralised and cynical about the intentions of the management.

Oldies versus Newies—this scenario can present a real headache and form a major buffer to a rebuilding program. When there is a core of people in a team who have been there quite a while, and then there is an influx of new graduates, for

example, there can be two quite distinct camps set up—the 'older cynical, been there before' group, and the 'young, enthusiastic, this is a wonderful opportunity' group, each group believing the other has lost the plot!

Assisting others to cope with change can be both a very rewarding and very frustrating experience. However, if carried out in the manner described above, the rewards and personal fulfilment can be immense.

SUMMARY

◆ When helping others to cope, remember the hints for spouses or partners, friends, and managers and supervisors.

◆ Assist individuals to handle change (recover, refocus, regenerate).

◆ Assist groups or teams to handle change. They will need assistance during the four phases of the change spiral.

◆ Consider the following factors when helping others to cope:

   - individuality;

   - hiccups and regressions; and

   - oldies versus newies.

CHAPTER 9

Living with a poor coper

Living with a poor coper can be an extremely frustrating situation, especially if you are very adaptive and stimulated by change and novelty in life. The person you live with and are close to may, however, see change as very threatening and unnerving. So what do you do? There are of course adaptive and maladaptive ways of trying to assist the person in being more attracted to change rather than resisting it.

CASE STUDY

Elsa was a teacher. She and Brenton had been married for 23 years. Brenton worked for a large telecommunications company and had been there since he was 17 years old. Two years ago, the company had restructured and Brenton was placed in a totally new role in a different department. He adapted badly, became very unsure of himself and seemed quite depressed. He withdrew from many activities that he had previously enjoyed and began drinking more alcohol through the week.

He refused to talk to Elsa about how he was feeling, only stating that he would never trust anyone again and that 'all the wind had been knocked out of his sails'.

CASE STUDY

Adam had been married to Kim for seven years and they had two sons before they divorced some five years ago. Adam often complained to his new partner Julie, of his ex-wife's treatment of him since the divorce, and how she had turned their sons against him. Julie had believed that once they moved in together, his focus would be more and more on their future. Not so! The complaints about his ex-wife continued and in fact seemed to increase, possibly because they were now spending more and more time together. Julie was at her wits' end and actually considered ending the relationship.

The effects of living with someone who cannot cope with change will vary greatly depending on the make-up and personal characteristics of the person. Let's look at some of the effects that living with a poor coper can have:

STRAIN ON THE PARTNERSHIP

Some people join with the poor coper in taking the easy road out and agreeing that the changes are silly, unnecessary and yes, they ought to be upset by what has happened.

FATIGUE

You can become worn out by the constant bitching, groaning and moaning from the person and from your constant efforts in trying to support the person and help him or her rationalise the situation, while at the same time dealing with your daily issues.

RESENTMENT, BLAMING AND ANGER

This is quite common, especially if you believe your lifestyle has been interfered with by the person's attitudes and behaviour regarding change. The lifestyle interference may come about because of the person's refusal to try new and exciting things in life, as a consequence of the fear of moving out of a comfort zone.

SYMPATHY

This can lead to a 'rescuing syndrome' where you spend abnormal amounts of time and effort trying to support and protect the person from the effects of the change. It can quite often end up with you feeling angry that you have put so much effort in, and you feel the person has not made a big enough effort to cope with the situation.

GUILT

The 'what's wrong with me' syndrome can also come into play. You may ask yourself 'why haven't I been able to assist?' Self-doubt may creep in—'do I really care for the person as much as I say I do? Have I tried to help enough? Could I do more, or should I be trying something different?'.

These are just a sample of the types of effects people who cope poorly with change can set up for the closest people in their lives to experience. So, if you live with that sort of person, you need to ensure you have good adaptive coping mechanisms so that you do not end up a victim in the whole affair.

SOME ADAPTIVE COPING TECHNIQUES

BEING WITH AND THEN DOING WITH

By this I mean being empathic and understanding of the person's plight, listening to how the person feels and how he or she has become affected by the change. The next step is to assist the person to find positive and adaptive solutions to what is happening. The first step is to *be with* the person, which is all about making sure you understand the person's feelings about what has happened. The second step is about *doing with* the person, which is the action phase and consists of looking for appropriate solutions.

HOW TO BE WITH THE PERSON

You need to allow sufficient time and discussion on the point or points raised by the person to try and understand where the person is coming from. This means employing good active listening skills:

♦ *listening*—paying attention, maintaining eye contact, remaining relaxed;

♦ *clarifying*—providing feedback to the person on what you think you have heard;

♦ *levelling*—being as honest as you can with the person about how you feel. This may help the person get a more realistic and positive perspective on the issue.

When we use the skills just mentioned it is less likely that we will quickly go into one of the responses mentioned earlier which may not be all that constructive for the person.

A word of caution—during this phase of *being with,* do not get into moralising or bringing value judgments down on the person or trying to rationalise by saying things like 'but don't you think . . .', 'you shouldn't think that way', 'but they have done so much for you' or 'what you should do is . . .' Once you feel you

understand where the person is coming from and you have spent enough time being with the person, move on to *doing with*.

HOW TO DO WITH THE PERSON

This is where you move on the action plan. In being with the person you gathered the facts. Now it's time to work with the person to find a solution to the worry, to allay concern about the change and to try and develop an *attraction to the change*.

There is generally little point in travelling down the path of arguing the facts or getting into almost appealing for a more positive view of the matter such as 'yes, but don't you think . . .' or 'wouldn't you agree that . . .', etc. The *doing with* phase focuses on helping the person to formulate an action plan which will help to alleviate the fear, anxiety or anger that may have developed. This means assisting the person to find solutions.

Remember, you do not want to rescue the person and run the risk of pushing him or her into a dependency trap. You are trying to help the person to gain ownership over the concerns by developing effective action plans so that he or she feel as much control over what is happening as possible.

Once an action plan has been formulated, you may be able to act as a support for the person in getting started and completing the steps in the plan. The technique briefly outlined next will be extremely useful. Remember to take every opportunity to reinforce and encourage the person. Praise solutions they come up with and begin to implement. Someone who has developed a 'poor me' syndrome over time or who is really in the victim trap may find it difficult to become more positive and solution-oriented. Here is the outline of an *effective problem-solving* technique:

◆ What is the challenge here?

◆ How does the person feel about it?

◆ Relax, take a short break.

◆ Consider all solutions.

◆ How might others resolve this situation?

◆ Put your solutions in order of worst to best.

◆ Select a solution.

◆ Formulate a plan of action to implement the solution.

◆ Set a starting date.

◆ Give yourself a pat on the back.

This has been a quick overview of the problem-solving procedure described in more detail in Chapter 7 which will greatly assist someone in seeing that there is indeed a positive solution to whatever is happening in their lives. It is a very good idea to work through the steps on paper so that people can see the process and solution unfold before their eyes. This will be a very good learning experience for situations that may happen in the future, and will equip people to deal with them more effectively and without so much emotional upheaval.

LOOKING AFTER YOURSELF

Throughout this whole process it is important that you remember to look after yourself.

Making sure that you keep the activities in your life going that are important to you. If you become too engrossed in the other person's problems you can become distracted from the things in your life that are important to you. You may then end up very angry and bitter towards the person, and seeing them as responsible for your life being in a minor chaos. You need to take responsibility for keeping your lifestyle intact, so keep those social, leisure and recreational pursuits in a good balance.

PROFESSIONAL COUNSELLING AND ASSISTANCE

When you feel you have exhausted your advice and assistance, or if the challenge is such that you really do not know where to go with it, then it is time to suggest that the person seek some professional guidance and advice. This option is explored more fully in Chapter 12.

WHEN ENOUGH IS ENOUGH

At times when all else has been tried, there may come a point when enough is enough. You need to decide when that is. If your own quality of life is being constantly eroded by someone remaining a victim to change or being very resistant to change, you may have to remove yourself from that situation.

It is your responsibility to take ownership of your own destiny, including surrounding yourself with positive thinking people and keeping a reasonable balance of activities in your life. If you don't do this, you may end up a victim in the whole affair, even when you initially started off as a helper.

An indication that you really do need to be careful is when you decide to give up and join the person in the victim trap or 'poor me' syndrome, and give in because the hassles are just not worth it. You may then stop doing things you enjoy, or stop planning things because they never appear to eventuate, or because they become too much of a hassle when you try to involve the person who is not coping well at all.

As stated earlier, encouraging the person to seek professional help is always a very useful and recommended option. Another option is to seek advice and counselling for yourself if you feel rather helpless about changing the situation.

Relationship counselling may also be a very real option to assist both of you in coping better and to prompt an honest reflection on problems.

CHECKLIST—ACTION PLAN

Do I live with someone who is resistant to change?

_____

How does this person resist the change?

_____

How does it affect me?

_____

How have I been dealing with it?

_____

What do I need to do?

_____

How will I know if I've been successful?

_____

SUMMARY

- Effects of living with a poor coper include:
  - strain on the partnership;
  - fatigue;
  - resentment, blaming, anger;
  - sympathy;
  - guilt.
- Use these adaptive coping techniques:
  - being with then doing with;
  - looking after yourself;
  - professional counselling and assistance;
  - when enough is enough.
- Refer to the checklist and action plan.

CHAPTER 10

You know you're coping well when . . .

This is an extremely important chapter because it helps us to troubleshoot how we are going in terms of coping well with, and adapting to, changes or likely changes in our lives. Dealing effectively with change in life can, and indeed, ought to be a great feeling. Success in any form is a wonderful thing. It enhances our self-esteem, self-confidence and self-dignity. One of the major benefits is the feedback that yes, we can achieve and cope with many things that life will hand out to us as we travel the journey.

Overcoming a 'resistance to change' habit is no different. We need to give ourselves a well-earned pat on the back for sticking at it and working through the issues and techniques involved.

So how do we know if we have been and are being successful in developing more of an attraction to change and in

implementing a far more rational, positive, and solution-oriented approach to change in life? The following pointers will give you a fairly accurate picture of just how successful you are being or have been.

Use the pointers as a guide. If you have done well, keep whatever it is you are doing going. If you have not done as well as you would have liked, don't get discouraged. Re-organise yourself, and re-read the relevant chapters of this book again doing the exercises as you go. People vary in how quickly they get used to the techniques and how successful they are in implementing them. Remember the old saying 'practice makes perfect', so keep at it.

SUCCESS POINTERS

WELL-BEING

An overall sense of well-being is a very good sign that you are on top of coping effectively with changes in your life. Well-being is best defined as a feeling of physical and emotional good health. So a bounce in your step, relaxed body—and body language, a smile on your face, and a perception of your own good health are pretty sure indicators.

HUMOUR

Being preoccupied with how terrible and awful particular changes in your life might be, even something as fundamental as growing older, is a very effective way to dampen and destroy your sense of humour and the ability to see the funny and light-hearted side of life. Humour is a great buffer against all sorts of possible stressors in life. It is also a fairly sure way of making and keeping friends. When our sense of humour starts to return we can rest assured that we are beginning

to get a handle on the change or changes we are facing. A sign that we are really coping well is the ability to laugh at ourselves and the silly little things that we do as we travel through life.

This generally indicates that we are not preoccupied with how terrible and awful things are or might become, or of things having to go our way at all times in life which, of course, is an impossibility.

SELF-ESTEEM

Do you have a positive self-image? Do you see yourself as an okay person and focus on what you have done, and can do, in life without being preoccupied with what you haven't done and what you can't do? Can you accept yourself, warts and all? Do you readily give yourself a pat on your back for a job well done? Can you admit mistakes without becoming all defensive? Do you feel free to be yourself, who you are, without excessive approval seeking or withdrawing from situations?

If you answered 'yes' or 'I do' to most of these questions or statements you have the changes where they need to be—under your control.

SELF-TALK

Are the messages coming out of that tape recorder in your head flexible, adaptable, rational, positive and solution-oriented?— remember to keep FARPSing. Do you think about the positive things that are happening in your life and in the world generally? Do you focus on the positive attributes of people, your manager, growing older, and the benefits and services your organisation provides for you?—after all they did give you a job and there is no universal law saying they had to.

If your self-talk (what you say to yourself about what is happening) is positive and optimistic, then there is a very good chance that you are coping very well with what is happening. Our self-talk tends to quickly become negative and upsetting if we are not coping very well.

RELATIONSHIPS

How at ease and relaxed we feel around others can indicate our level of coping, especially when accompanied by some of the other pointers. Are you understanding, accepting and patient with others? Do you take an interest in what others are doing? Can you be supportive and understanding of what others might be coping with? Can you form close intimate relationships easily and do you maintain these over time? Do you speak and converse with people in a manner that encourages them to trust you, to do their best and which allows them to speak their minds? Are you predictable and even-tempered when dealing with others?

POSITIVE HABITS

Ongoing sustained positive habits are very good indicators that all is well in life and that we are maintaining a focus on looking after ourselves and balancing the activities in our lives well.

Positive habits include:

◆ moderate to low levels of alcohol intake;

◆ a balanced low fat diet;

◆ regular exercise;

◆ reasonable work hours;

◆ limited cups of coffee per day;

◆ no smoking;

◆ regular passive and active relaxation pursuits;

◆ making time for ourselves.

NOVELTY VS. COMFORT ZONE

Human beings thrive on a certain amount of risk-taking. Those who don't are more predisposed to heightened anxiety and depressive disorders.

If we do not take certain risks and have some novelty in our lives we can begin to 'rust out', which is characterised by feeling understimulated, lethargic and bored. When this happens we can turn to negative addictions to cope.

When we feel able to let go of or step outside of our comfort zones and have a go, we have a very good chance of enjoying and managing changes effectively. Not only do we cope with changes in life much better, we also enhance our overall quality of life. Now that you have had time to consider these issues, complete the following checklist and see how you fare.

CONTROLLING OUR REACTIONS TO CHANGE—A CHECKLIST

Response:	yes	no
I generally feel in good health.	____	____
I find I smile a lot.	____	____
If I make a silly mistake my first reaction is to laugh at it.	____	____
I often laugh and smile about things in life.	____	____
I like to get close to other people.	____	____
I give tasks in life my best shot.	____	____
I know I am a worthwhile person.	____	____
I have enough close friends.	____	____
I have no more than 24 alcoholics drinks (men)/ 14 alcoholic drinks (women) per week.	____	____
I am a normal weight for my height.	____	____
New and different things generally excite me.	____	____
With proper planning I can deal with anything.	____	____
I generally think 'I can do it'.	____	____
There are a lot of wonderful positive things happening in the world.	____	____

Response: yes   no

I don't allow myself to stay bored for too long.   _____   _____

It's challenging and exciting to push yourself
that extra step.   _____   _____

I enjoy my own company.   _____   _____

I am not unduly concerned about death.   _____   _____

I believe life is here to be enjoyed.   _____   _____

HOW TO INTERPRET YOUR SCORE

To score your profile, add up the number of *yes* answers.

15–20: Super effort—very well done and good on you. Your mission now is to maintain the positive attitudes and behaviours that have been working so effectively for you to date. Keep them going; work on them and troubleshoot as you need to. You are a great role model for others trying to cope with changes in their life.

10–14: You are certainly on your way and nearly there. With more practice and attention to the techniques in this book you will develop solutions to any minor blocks to you coping effectively with change. Make sure you keep a focus on solutions and make sure you practise—it is worth it.

5–9: You have just left the launch pad. There is still quite a distance to travel, but take heart, at least you're airborne. You know where you want to get to, and now you will have extra ideas and solutions to help you get there. Remember to practise, practise, practise, Rome wasn't built in a day! Don't let anything divert you from your course.

0–4: You need to go back to Chapter 1 and read through the book again making sure you do the exercises as you go. It really is quite easy to get the hang of the techniques and solutions I have gone over—it is just a matter of developing *stickability* and not giving up on it. Start with the attitude that says 'I am important to look after'. If you continue to feel lost and a victim to change, seriously consider getting some professional advice and help for yourself (see Chapter 12). Good luck and keep at it.

It really is important to have a high quality of life and to feel that yes, certain changes in life may be a pain in the butt, but you can handle them and give life your best shot. Not being able to accept or deal effectively with changes will most certainly interfere with your journey through life. If you find you just can't get there by using your own resources, then seek professional advice, assistance and/or counselling.

SUMMARY

◆ The success pointers are:
  – well-being;
  – humour;
  – self-esteem;
  – positive self-talk;
  – positive relationships;
  – positive habits;
  – a balance of novelty and comfort zone in your life.
◆ Controlling our reactions to change—a checklist—how did you fare?

CHAPTER 11

Memory joggers — personal action plan

This chapter serves as a memory jogger for the important aspects and issues that have been discussed in the previous chapters, and that I feel are worthy of quickly revisiting to make sure we have our ideas and techniques in order.

The idea is to see how many of the questions or statements posed you can come up with answers for. You can then check each answer with the relevant chapter by chapter if you need to. Pencil in those answers which you had difficulty with. Enjoy the challenge!

SORTING OUT CHANGE

1. Is change a new phenomenon?

_____

_____

_____

2. What are the common changes we face during our lifetime?

_____

_____

_____

_____

3. Why the need for change—is it necessary or not?

_____

_____

_____

_____

4. What are the phases of the change spiral?

_____

_____

_____

_____

5. What are the five stages of change readiness?

_____

_____

_____

6. How did you fare on the change quiz—are your ready or not?
   Why or why not?

_____

_____

_____

7. Describe the difference between an owner and a victim when it comes to dealing with change.

_____

_____

_____

_____

8. What are the four categories any event in life can fall into, and what are the four possible sets of skills we can use to cope with the changes they may bring?

_____

_____

_____

_____

9. What are the 3Rs of effective coping following a reasonable change in our lives?

_____

_____

_____

_____

10. What is meant by emotional maturity?

_____

_____

_____

_____

11. Describe briefly a quick relaxation technique you can use.

_____

_____

_____

_____

12. What is attitudinal efficiency and FARPsing?

_____

_____

_____

_____

13. List down the 10 points for effective problem-solving.

_____

_____

_____

_____

14. What are some important considerations when helping others to cope, both individually and in groups or teams?

_____

_____

_____

_____

15. The important aspects of living with a poor coper are:

_____

_____

_____

16. What are the signs of coping well?

_____

_____

_____

_____

PERSONAL ACTION PLAN

1. Is there a particular change in your life you need to cope with now? What is it, or are they?

_____

_____

2. What are the important things you need to do to cope effectively?

_____

_____

3. How will you know when you are successful?

_____

_____

4. A reward I will give myself for coping effectively is:

_____

_____

Well done. It's important to take the time to help yourself, and also to become a positive and stimulating person for others to be around. At the end of the day its all about stickability and doing the right things right.

CHAPTER 12

Sources of assistance and how to get the most from counselling

HY SEEK PROFESSIONAL HELP?

If you feel you need more guidance or extra assistance in dealing and coping with change or changes in your life, then do it. Professional advice and counselling is for people who decide they are important to look after and so they are going to take control over their lives—it is a very real sign of personal strength. It is not a sign of weakness or of being totally out of control. So, if following the reading of this book and exposure to the type of techniques necessary to break any 'change trap', you still need some extra assistance, then do it. All that remains then is to ensure you obtain the right advice, support or counselling. This means you need to know about the types of counsellors and assistance to seek, how to find it, and how to get the most from the sessions.

HOW TO GET THE MOST FROM THE COUNSELLING

When seeking counselling for any reason, there are a few things you need to keep in mind:

◆ choose a credible person to see, and remember, how much you get out of the counselling will depend on yourself;

- counsellors are certainly not healers, but they can *help you to help yourself*;
- all the counselling in the world is of little value, unless you practise what you learn;
- counselling is an opportunity to learn, not just to be proven right;
- if there are particular important issues you wish to discuss with the counsellor, make sure you write them down and take them with you so you do not forget;
- take notes during the session if you wish;
- it is your right to seek a second opinion if you wish;
- keep an open mind when attending the counselling;
- make sure you get clarification on issues you are unsure of.

CHOOSING ASSISTANCE—WHO DO I NEED TO SEE?

Make sure the psychologist you choose is registered in your State. The State registration board will be able to tell you if a particular person is registered or not. Beware that some practitioners can place ads in the yellow pages and call themselves counsellors or psychologists without any qualifications or professional ethics at all. To assist you in coping with change in your life, you need to try and find a clinical psychologist who is trained in what are termed the cognitive-behavioural forms of counselling and therapy. These psychologists are generally in private practice or work for Community Health Services or large hospitals.

This particular style of advice, counselling and therapy is aimed at making sure we learn how to think and develop attitudes that are positive, rational and solution-oriented. This will then have a very positive impact on our behavioural and emotional state.

HOW DO YOU FIND A PSYCHOLOGIST?

Psychologists are located under 'P' in the yellow pages. These are generally psychologists in private practice, so you will pay for their services. Fees vary from around $60 to $145 per session. The fee recommended by the Australian Psychological Society per hour session was around $145 at the time this book was published. To check, you can always call the society on Freecall 1800 333 497. Remember, sometimes you really do get what you pay for!

Community Health Centres, mental health teams and your local large hospital may also have psychologists on staff who provide services to the general community. These services are generally free. Some of these facilities also provide group stress management, assertiveness and relaxation sessions. If you find yourself in a desperate situation, overwhelmed by concern late at night, services such as Lifeline can be excellent in an emergency, and you will find a list of the Community Services in the beginning of the white pages of the phone book. Your local or family general practitioner will also be able to refer you to a well-regarded psychologist.

BEWARE!

MEDICATION

Prescribed medications may help in the short-term if you are overcome by sudden unexpected major happenings or loss in your life. If taken for long periods of time, you can develop both a physiological and a psychological addiction or dependency on them. The effects of these dependencies are often worse than the original problem, so be cautious. If a medical practitioner or psychiatrist has you on medication discuss this with them regularly, and get a referral to someone who can guide you in learning self-help techniques—generally a trained cognitive behavioural psychologist. If in doubt, get a second opinion. This is your right.

LONG-TERM PSYCHOANALYSIS

Generally speaking, long-term treatment of this nature can be expensive and not always effective. In my opinion, there are far more effective techniques for assisting people with coping problems, to which the research testifies quite clearly. Beware of the three times a week for two years types. If you are considering this option, it is definitely my advice to get a second opinion.

FRINGE DWELLERS

These are practitioners who deal in para-psychological techniques such as re-birthing, or repressed memory syndrome. In my opinion, treatments of this nature can foster dependency, drain your money and in some instances set you up to get involved with 'unusual' groups. These techniques can be delivered by groups who prey on the emotionally vulnerable, so be careful to check them out thoroughly.

Remember that you are important to look after. If you really need professional assistance, don't be afraid to seek it out.

The future will be what you make it. You need to develop an attraction to change because you really have no choice. Change will occur—whether it is growing older, someone close to you dying or retrenchment from a job. Trying to escape from the reality will only buy you some time. You need to meet change head on. It is not always pleasant but it is generally able to be dealt with and with the right attitude and actions it will generally turn out fine. All the very best.

FURTHER READING

Brecht, G., *Sorting out Goals*, Prentice Hall, Sydney, 1996

Brecht, G., *Sorting out Relationships*, Prentice Hall, Sydney, 1996

Brecht, G., *Sorting out Self-esteem*, Prentice Hall, Sydney, 1996

Brecht, G., *Sorting out Stress*, Prentice Hall, Sydney, 1996

Brecht, G., *Sorting out Worry*, Prentice Hall, Sydney, 1996

Ellis, A., *How to stubbornly refuse to make yourself miserable about anything, yes, anything!* Pan Macmillan, Sydney, 1991.

Mackay, H., *Reinventing Australia: The Mind of Australia in the 90s*, HarperCollins Publishers, Sydney, 1993.

Seligman, M., *What You Can Change and What You Can't: The Complete Guide to Successful Self-improvement*, Random House, Sydney, 1994.

INDEX

living with a poor coper,
96–103
success pointer, 107
relaxation, 107, 118
relaxation technique, 55–57
'rescuing' syndrome, 98
resentment, 98
retrenchment, 79, 90–91
risk-taking, 107
roles
ageing and, 8
helping others to cope, 89–95

self-dignity
ageing and, 9
self-esteem, 52, 54, 72, 91
ageing and, 9
success pointer, 106
self-talk, 47, 54
irrational beliefs, 63–65, 70
success pointer, 106
shock, 20, 79
social changes, 11
solutions to change, 40
spouses
grieving, 89–90
living with a poor coper,
96–103
relationship breakdowns, 91
retrenchment, 90
success indicators, 104–110
supervisors
assisting with change, 92–95
helping with grieving, 90

helping with relationship
breakdowns, 91
helping with retrenchment, 90
sympathy, 98

teams
coping with change, 92–95
techniques to cope with change
adaptive attitudes, 69–73
attitudinal efficiency, 57–61
catastrophe scale, 73–74
focusing, 52, 54
living with a poor coper,
98–102
relaxation, 55–57
thought stopping and switching, 65–67, 72, 74
technological changes, 10, 14
thought stopping and switching, 65–67,
72, 74
thoughts
distorted, 63–65
negative, 52–53
positive, 48, 53, 72

victim mentality, 14, 34–39
victim trap, 48, 81, 84, 90, 100, 102
visualising, 73

well-being, 105
work changes, 2, 10–11
redundancies, 27
retrenchment, 79, 90–91
work hours, 107
work practices, 11